YOU FIRST

INSPIRE YOUR TEAM TO GROW UP,
GET ALONG, AND GET STUFF DONE

LIANE DAVEY

WILEY

For general information about our other products and services, please contact our Customer
Care Department within the United States at (800) 762–2974, outside the United States
at (317) 572–3993 or fax (317) 572–4002.

Wiley publishes in a variety of print and electronic formats and by print-on-demand. Some
material included with standard print versions of this book may not be included in e-books or in
print-on-demand. If this book refers to media such as a CD or DVD that is not included in the
version you purchased, you may download this material at http://booksupport.wiley.com.
For more information about Wiley products, visit www.wiley.com.

Library of Congress Cataloging-in-Publication Data:

Davey, Liane Margaret, 1972-
   You first : inspire your team to grow up, get along, and get stuff done / Liane Davey.
      pages cm
   Includes bibliographical references.
   ISBN 978-1-118-63670-1 (cloth); ISBN 978-1-118-71492-8 (ebk);
ISBN 978-1-118-71475-1 (ebk); ISBN 978-1-118-71479-9 (ebk)
1.   Teams in the workplace—Management. 2.   Employee motivation. 3.   Organizational
behavior. 4.   Interpersonal relations.   I. Title.
   HD66.D376'2013
   658.4'022—dc23

                                                                              2013011038

Printed in the United States of America

10   9   8   7   6   5   4   3   2   1

To the home team: Craig, Kira, and Mac

CONTENTS

CHAPTER 1

Change Yourself, Change Your Team

THE GREAT PROMISE OF TEAMS

> "A team can make better decisions, solve more complex problems, and do more to enhance creativity and build skills than individuals working alone. . . . They have become the vehicle for moving organizations into the future. . . . Teams are not just nice to have. They are hard-core units of the production."
> —Blanchard[1]

Better decisions, increased productivity, and heightened engagement: Teams promise a lot. At their best, teams make many things easier. Good teams solve problems[2] better than individuals. They improve quality.[3] Teams can increase your engagement and motivation. One study of British rowers even found a physiological advantage to teamwork,[4] with team members releasing more endorphins than individuals rowing the same race. *We're wired for teamwork*.

Beyond any physical benefit, teams have an intellectual advantage because they make more information available to you, help you generate more novel ideas, and give you access to more people who can identify good ideas—and weed out bad ones.

But the proof of the benefits of teamwork isn't just in the numbers. If you've experienced at least one strong team in your career, you know the feeling in your gut. Being part of a great team is electric. You feel more connected, you feel the upward spiral of ideas getting better and better. You know that a bunch of people have your back. It's easy to get stuff done. Once you've felt what it's like to be on a truly great team, you'll always want that feeling back.

That's the feeling you're trying to evoke when you plaster the office walls with cheery posters of mountain climbers, rowers, and planes flying in formation.

The Sad Reality of Teams

For many people today, the reality of working on a team is nothing like what's shown in those posters. Teams can feel pretty crappy. Instead of collaboration, you're in competition with your colleagues. Instead of diversity of thought and breadth of ideas, there's tunnel vision. Instead of friendship and camaraderie, there's gossip and backstabbing.

And it's not as though the pain is all worth it because you're so much more productive. In many instances, teams are slower and less productive than individuals. Seriously? All that drama for nothing! Teams aren't even more accurate than individuals. And that promise of increased engagement and motivation goes out the window when lack of role clarity, mistrust, and unhealthy conflict sour your relationships. Research has even debunked the value of the corner-stone of teamwork—the brainstorming session.[5] *Teams are failing us.*

Teams Are Here to Stay

There's no going back to a world where we all did most of our work independently. Teams have multiplied as our work has grown more complicated. If you go way back to 77 AD, one man—Pliny the Elder—managed to write an encyclopedia of all that was known to mankind. Today, that's just impossible to fathom! No single person could possibly know all there is to know even in one very specific field. *We can't know enough without teams.*

The huge increase in the use of teams is also part of a seismic cultural change. Command and control organizations didn't need teams to get things done—they had *memoranda*. The boss sent out a memo and everyone got on board. "Yes, sir, right away, sir!" When was the last time you saw a memo? Today, our organizational cultures are more sensitive to engagement and buy-in. We have to use influence instead of authority to get things done. Meetings have replaced memos. *We can't get things done without teams*.

I recently reached out to human resources leaders in 50 large and midsized organizations and asked them whether teams would be less, equally, or more important in the future than they are today. Eighty-nine percent of respondents said that teams would be more (or much more) important in the future. *Teams are here to stay*.

Teams are the way work gets done in our increasingly complex, fast-paced, global world. They are the basic unit of our organizations and a critical piece of the productivity puzzle. For many of us, our work teams are also the closest thing we have to community in our urban, disconnected, two-hour-commute lives. My teammates are my colleagues, my sounding boards, my friends, and even the aunties and uncles to my two daughters. For both our organizations and ourselves, there is a lot riding on our ability to make teams work.

What I've Learned about Fixing Teams

The problems facing teams are serious, but instead of fixing the serious teamwork problems with serious solutions, most team-building sessions focus on fun or frivolous activities like cooking classes or white-water rafting. I guess the idea is that if you can have fun outside the office, maybe you can recapture the fun back in the office. Unfortunately, it doesn't work that way.

More often than not, people return with horror stories about team issues being magnified by these types of sessions. The cooking class highlights how your team can't get its act together and ends with everyone eating a cold meal just to rub their noses in it. The karaoke night widens the gap that already exists between the outgoing party types and the more hesitant introverts. The Popsicle-stick boat sinks along with your hopes of building a better team. Expecting silly exercises to fix serious issues is ridiculous.

On the other side of the spectrum are the "tissue issue" team builders. These are the team-building facilitators who think that if you remove the tables, sit in a circle, and have an authentic dialogue with one another that everything will be fine. These folks come prepared with their box of tissues because they don't feel like they've created a breakthrough until someone cries. These sessions can make things a whole lot worse in a hurry. It's just not acceptable that these are your only options when you want to invest in your team.

For the last 17 years, I've been studying and working with teams. I started back when I was a graduate student in psychology studying the dynamics that affect innovation in high-tech product development teams. That research was my first evidence of the profound connection between team effectiveness and business success. For the past decade, I've been working as an advisor to executive teams. At first, I focused mostly on facilitating strategy, but it didn't take long for me to learn that the quality of the strategy process hinged on the dynamics of the team. For the past 7 years I've been helping top teams improve their alignment to strategy, reduce their dysfunction, and fulfill the promise of teamwork in creating productive organizations.

By the time I get a call to help a team, things are usually pretty bad. Some teams openly admit the severity of the problem. But many try to downplay their distress. They say things like, *"We're a good team, and we're just trying to become a great team."* It doesn't take long to learn that the *patient* is in bad shape. Sure, they're walking and talking, getting things done, but they've got badly blocked arteries, and the only solution is the team equivalent of open-heart surgery. That's how I spend most of my days. I wheel teams into the operating room, crack them open, and try to repair the damage. But it doesn't have to be that way.

Just like eating well and exercising every day can greatly reduce the risk of heart disease, simple, healthy practices on a team can prevent or at least reduce the impact of the most common team dysfunctions. If you get into the habit of doing these small things every day, you'll prevent your team from becoming dysfunctional.

These steps are more effective than gimmicky team-building programs. Going on a rock-climbing retreat to solve your team's problems is like trying to get healthy with diet shakes and a Thigh-Master. Living up to the responsibilities outlined in this book will prevent your team from reaching a crisis point where you need to invest in a costly team intervention.

THERE'S ONE CATCH

I sat across the table from the vice president of human resources of a large manufacturer. I hadn't worked with his team before, but from the interviews I had done with the members, I could tell things weren't good. The team was micromanaging and spending too much time in the weeds. They were also trapped in a bad dynamic where most members didn't trust, or even like, one another. I wasn't the first expert they'd hired to help.

I met with him to go over what I'd heard in the one-on-one interviews and get ready for the session. As we sat in his office, we stared out the windows at the water in silence until he said what we were both thinking: "This has to work. We won't get another chance."

Unfortunately, he thought that statement was about me. I was the team effectiveness expert, and I needed to fix the team. I needed to stop their yelling. I needed to cure their mistrust. I needed to make them forgive past indiscretions and move forward with a clean slate.

I can't fix a team. No team expert, no matter how skilled, can. You see, my secret weapon isn't a magic wand—it's a mirror. No matter how badly I want to cure a team, all I can do is create the conditions for the team to cure itself. I told the VP of HR what I tell every client: I'll give you everything you need to understand how and why you need to change. But you have to make the change yourselves.

Each and every team I've seen recover from dysfunction has been led by one brave soul who looked in the mirror and didn't like what he or she saw. And instead of waiting for everyone else to change, that person decided to go first. Each and every team that got healthy had one member who would trust without being trusted. One person who would respond to hostility with curiosity. One person who would stand up for the teammate who others were shutting down.

If you are willing to be that person on your team, congratulations. If you are ready to make a change, this book will be your inspiration for why to try, your handbook for how to do it, and your measuring stick for how you're doing.

> Are you ready to change your team?

THE ROAD AHEAD

In the first half of this book, the section on Toxic Teams, you will diagnose what's going on in your team. I'll introduce the most common team diseases and share the early warning signs, the symptoms, and some things you can do—even without the support of your colleagues or team leader—to get your team back on the right path. By the end of the Toxic Teams section, you'll be tuned in to the dynamics that are at play on your team. You'll know if your team is at risk of becoming one of the following:

Crisis Junkie team: Stalled by unclear priorities, lack of role clarity, and political infighting, the Crisis Junkie team lurches through life in search of the next crisis that will unite it with a common goal, unlock resources, and stop the petty bickering.

Bobble Head team: Homogenized by shared values, perspectives, and experiences, the Bobble Head team goes with the flow but maintains harmony, at the cost of little innovation and dangerous detachment from the risks of its decisions.

Spectator team: Fragmented by members who check out of discussions, the Spectator team loses the benefit of diverse perspectives and sinks into apathy that ensures the whole will never be greater than the sum of its parts.

Bleeding Back team: Plagued by underground conflict and back-channel decision making, the Bleeding Back team nods its head in public and puts up a fight in private, causing a perpetual loop of one step forward and two steps back.

Royal Rumble team: Scarred by vicious attacks, screaming fits, and personal agendas, the Royal Rumble team fails to harness passion and instead spends all its time going back and forth and none of its time moving forward.

In the second half of the book, you'll learn the daily regimen you can use to keep your team healthy or to start fixing your team if it's broken. No single tactic will cure a Toxic Team, but if you live up to each of the following five responsibilities, you can cure every one of the different dysfunctions. Each of the responsibilities is simple in theory and difficult in practice. When applied, each will have a profound impact on your team and on you. It doesn't matter where you sit at the table; every team member can and should live up to these five responsibilities:

Start with a Positive Assumption: Short-circuit your biases, unpack your baggage, and truly appreciate the value that your teammates are bringing.

Add Your Full Value: Show up, get off cruise control, and bring the benefit of your experiences, your relationships, and your personality instead of just doing what is in your job description.

Amplify Other Voices: Loan your credibility and your airtime to teammates whose minority perspectives are usually shut out of the discussion.

Know When to Say "No": Retrain yourself when and how to say no to the things that would dilute your focus, stretch your resources, and slow you down.

Embrace Productive Conflict: Tap into the value of different points of view by disagreeing about the issues in a way that promotes understanding and reduces defensiveness.

Change Your Team

Teams are the way we get work done. Organizations need teams to live up to their promise instead of getting mired in dysfunction. Getting teams healthy will pay off richly in terms of productivity, innovation, and risk management.

But productivity, innovation, and risk management all pale in comparison to the true reason we need our teams healthy. Unhealthy Toxic Teams make our working lives miserable. Stress in the workplace costs our economy billions of dollars, and it's costing you what are supposed to be the best years of your life. You know what it's like: two hours into the team meeting and that one guy is droning on and on without listening to anyone, and you want to strangle him. You're spending hundreds of dollars on pain relievers and massages just to deal with the tension.

And it's almost impossible to leave a Toxic Team at the office. You carry the stress and anxiety with you when you walk through the door at home. You are distracted at dinner, quick-tempered with your partner, and harsh with your kids. It has to stop.

I'm passionate about teams because I have experienced the misery of working on a Toxic Team. Early in my career, I was a member of a Toxic Team. I kept on downplaying the effect our team leader was having on me until one day I saw a speech given by Dr. John Izzo. I am eternally grateful to him, because he gave me the kick in the pants I needed to get out of that environment. He said, "Every day, everywhere you go, you spread a virus. You decide if that virus is positive or negative." I realized that the toxic environment on the team had poisoned me. Just walking into the office made me grouchy. I spent more time complaining than making things better. I was spreading a negative virus.

Twenty-six days later, I submitted my resignation. It took me about two months to really appreciate the terrible toll that team had taken on me. I realized I had been wasting all my energy trying to protect myself from the team leader's wicked accusations, and I had no energy left for anything else.

I hadn't been doing my best work. I hadn't been the kind of colleague and mentor to my team that I should have been. Worse, I had carried the weight of the day home with me at night. My daughter would ask to walk to the park or ride her tricycle, and I would tell her I was too tired and switch on the television to placate her, something I had sworn to myself I would never do.

Since that moment eight years ago, I've been committed to doing my part to end the misery of bad teams. I've learned that Toxic Teams are inefficient, they waste resources, and they leave people feeling unproductive, disengaged, and exhausted. No one deserves to feel that way.

I left my Toxic Team, but you don't have to. You can change your team from the inside. One person—no matter where you sit— one person can change the trajectory of a whole team. Starting to behave differently, to unpack your baggage, and to disagree positively will make it easier for your teammates to do the same. Good behavior from you will encourage good behavior from others, and you'll be amazed how much better things will be. If you have the courage, you can change your team.

If you change yourself, you will change your team.

CHAPTER 2

Toxic Teams

I was sitting at my desk, working away, when the phone rang. It was the CEO of a small financial organization.[1] He'd called a week before to ask about our work on team effectiveness, and I'd sent him some material on our Team Inoculation® program. We designed this program to help get new teams off on the right foot. We affectionately refer to it as the *flu shot* for teams because it's meant to immunize teams against common dysfunctions.

He didn't waste any time getting to the point on this second call. "Thanks for sending the material on the flu shot," he said. "I don't think that's going to cut it. Do you have a *rabies shot*?"

I immediately imagined a team of executives sitting around the table frothing at the mouth. It wasn't quite that bad, but it was pretty horrible. Members of the team had stopped trusting one another and communicating all but the most necessary information.

Before the first session, we interviewed the CEO, the board chair, and the entire executive team. They painted a pretty bleak picture. The organization used to be listed as one of the nation's best employers. Now engagement had plummeted. The most recent internal survey asked employees to agree or disagree with the statement "Our organization has the leadership we need to be successful." Not a single employee agreed. Not *one!*

No surprise that the business was in a downward spiral. Thanks to internal squabbles, the team couldn't deliver the tools the sales force needed to keep up with the increasingly tough competition. Sales had been falling for three years. There was no time to waste in getting this team back to health.

We had our first session at a really nice hotel surrounded by stunning views of a forested section of the city. Things inside weren't quite so picturesque. As members of the team arrived, they said hello to my colleague, Bryan, and me, but ignored each other, burying their heads in newspapers or their smartphones.

We took it slowly for the first day. We knew we'd need to build trust before we could get at what was really going on. We started by talking about the purpose of the organization because it was something everyone felt strongly about and could agree on. They came to some valuable conclusions about what their team should be focused on. By the end of the day, they were comfortable enough to express some of their frustration: *"This was all well and good, but we didn't talk about what's wrong. We need to talk about what's not working."* They wanted to point fingers, to blame someone, to unleash their emotions. But they weren't ready to do that without making things much, much worse.

In our second session, we used an assessment tool to help the team understand the feelings behind their coworkers' behavior and set them up for the difficult conversations they needed to have. By session three, we were ready to delve into the issues. And boy, were there issues. The members of this team were walking wounded.

Everyone on the team had significant grievances. They felt wronged, and they wanted to see public trials for the offending teammates. I think most of them were expecting Bryan and me to pronounce judgment on the offenders right there in the session. The alleged crimes varied. Some had been caught telling people that their teammates didn't know how to do their jobs. One vice president had instructed her direct reports to ignore instructions from one of the other VPs. Another refused to share an important document with a colleague because she didn't trust her with the sensitive material. Even the CEO was in on the action, asking the board to let him terminate the CFO without addressing the issues directly with him.

We saw anger, frustration, and distress. And not just in the boardroom. The executive team's direct reports took the brunt of the conflict when they were asked to ignore or question their peers and thus spread the misery in the organization. Of course, this dysfunction affected team members' sleep, appetite, and health. Their relationships and their families suffered. The whole situation had become toxic.

Toxic Teams: A team where the lack of alignment and the poor dynamic are a threat to both the productivity of the organization and to the engagement and well-being of individual members.

Toxic Teams are like cancers: The exact cause of the disease and the prognosis can vary widely. When you take diverse individuals and combine them into teams, you get infinite permutations of dysfunction. Some teams are dysfunctional from the start, thanks to immature, abusive, or conflict-avoidant individuals. Other teams work well until something sours the quality of their members' interactions. Even small changes in the membership or the context of the team can turn a normally healthy team into a dysfunctional one.

You know you're on a Toxic Team when:

- you dread going to work on Monday mornings (and Tuesdays, Wednesdays, and Thursdays)

- you work your butt off but face the same issues and problems time after time

- you go to the washroom on another floor to avoid Gossip Central

- you copy the boss and the boss's boss on every e-mail to cover your backside

- you're embarrassed to tell people which team you're on

Teams turn toxic when something goes wrong in one of two dimensions: the alignment or the dynamic.

Alignment

You know your team is aligned when you're focused on things that are important to the organization, you are each clear about your roles, and those roles complement one another instead of conflicting. Without alignment, it feels like you're just spinning your wheels.

You'll find yourself in a Toxic Team if there is too little alignment because you'll either be dropping balls ("That wasn't my responsibility") or stepping on one another's toes ("That's MY turf!"). A team with poor alignment wastes a lot of energy running off in all directions. If you often find yourself working and reworking projects or putting out fires, that's a sign that alignment is broken somewhere in the chain.

Okay, so a quick meeting to review the team's purpose should clear up any problems, right? Wrong. Your team can also turn toxic if there is too much alignment—when alignment becomes uniformity. When your team is too tightly aligned, there isn't enough diversity of thought to trigger innovation or expose underlying risk. At the extreme, every team member is thinking exactly the same thing. You might as well just have one person work on the problem alone. You might be surprised how often over-alignment is the problem on teams.

Getting alignment right means finding that sweet spot where everybody's thinking independently, but still working toward a common purpose. Each of the Toxic Teams that I will describe in the following chapters has gotten this balance wrong somehow. Two team types in particular have alignment issues at the heart of their dysfunction. Too little alignment is the fundamental problem of a Crisis Junkie team, and too much is the issue for Bobble Heads.

Dynamic

The other major issue is how your teammates interact with one another. You know you have a healthy dynamic when team members communicate openly, candidly, and respectfully. This contributes to high levels of trust and makes your team a mature and positive place to be. But a good dynamic isn't just valuable for its own sake; you'll see the impact of the dynamic on creativity, decision making, and execution. That's why a good dynamic is critical to the health of the team and the success of your organization.

A healthy dynamic has to be more than skin deep. I have heard many, many people claim to be on wonderful, healthy teams, only to find that the smiles mask serious problems. The desire to maintain harmonious relationships can make your team avoid difficult topics and gloss over issues that require hearty debate. If you're engaged and cheery but unwilling to go beyond a superficial view of the world, your team is as much of a risk to your organization as the team that devolves into fisticuffs. A counterproductive dynamic is a factor in every Toxic Team. It's a hallmark of a Spectator team, where there is too little conflict, and a Royal Rumble team, where there is too much.

How Sick Is Your Team?

You might already be reacting to the language I'm using to describe unhealthy teams. *"Sure, we might not be up for Team of the Year, but I don't think I'd say we're toxic!"* The term *toxic* makes a lot of people squeamish. Toxic doesn't mean your team is doomed!

Think about the word *toxic* and the idea of toxins. You're surrounded by toxic substances every day. They're usually not concentrated enough to knock you out. But you become less and less healthy as those toxins build in your body. The same is true of your team. Maybe your team isn't obviously sick yet, maybe you're still functioning fine, but are the toxins building up? Is it time to clean up your act so your team can stay healthy and productive for years to come?

Read the first half of this book with an open mind. You might not see a mirror image of any of the Toxic Teams when you look around your meeting room, but do you see hints that your team is starting to deteriorate? If you understand the origins of Toxic Teams, you can spot a problem before it really hampers your team.

If you do see your team reflected in the descriptions of the Toxic Teams, don't fret. Admitting that your team is unhealthy is nothing to be ashamed of. Few teams become dysfunctional intentionally or even knowingly. Your dysfunctional behavior is a natural response to the pressure you're under: the pressure to drop everything when a crisis strikes, the pressure to get along, to act civilly, to be engaged and passionate. You're expected to be all these things while your work is getting more complex, more interdependent, more urgent. The operative word is *more*. More, more, more!

Coping

So if you are like most of the team members I work with (heck, if you're like *me*), you make little compromises just to survive the day. You drop your opposition to an idea because the boss seems so committed to it. You let a nasty comment slide because the guy will ignore what you say anyway. You lob a personal attack at a colleague because it will scuttle their idea faster than trying to make a rational case. You take out your stress by gossiping with a teammate over coffee—what happens at Starbucks stays at Starbucks.

The first time you do any of these things, it's understandable and forgivable. You're under so much pressure, you're inevitably going to lose your temper or let something slide at some point. Cut yourself some slack. It's what you do the second time and the third time that matters. The second time you use a coping strategy, it's a pattern, and you need to get serious about doing the right thing instead of taking the easy way out. The third time, it's a habit, and you're already in trouble. The good news is that there is a way back.

It's time to dive in, figure out what's really going on, and start making it better. Here's how to do that.

In the following five chapters, I will take you on a tour of the most common types of Toxic Teams. We'll peek in the windows of their meetings, hide out behind their water coolers, and even listen in on the voices in their heads. You'll spot the normal, even desirable motives and behaviors that can actually set your team on a path to dysfunction. Then you'll see the peril that lies ahead if your team becomes toxic—the costs to your organization and to you personally. By that point, you might start to recognize some of the descriptions.

For each Toxic Team, there is a quick diagnostic quiz. Does your team have a full-blown version of the disease or just a few of the early warning signs? If you reflect on how your team behaves, can you confidently say that there is no risk of developing a particular problem? As you complete each diagnostic, tally your scores and get a sense of just how bad it is. You can feel good if you're only checking off one or two items in the Early Warning section. If, on the other hand, you're checking off the Moderate to Extreme symptoms in the lower sections of the quiz, you need to act quickly.

You might find that your team is particularly vulnerable to one toxic pattern. You might see some aspect of each of the Toxic Teams. Your team's dysfunction may vary depending on the particular situation or issue you're dealing with. There are as many ways for teams to be toxic as there are views through a kaleidoscope. And each shift in the world, the organization, or the membership of the team changes the picture.

This book isn't just about Toxic Teams; it's also about how to build healthy ones. Although the second half of the book will show you how to cure your team's dysfunction, you won't have to wait that long to get started. In each of the Toxic Team chapters, you'll find instructions for how to triage your situation and administer some emergency medicine. If you are the team leader, or if you've got your boss on board, you can make some formal and structural changes to hardwire good behavior.

Unfortunately, based on conversations with thousands of team members, I know that expecting your boss to be aware of and willing to do something about the issues might be overly optimistic. If you're on a team where the boss is contributing to the problem or at least determined to stay blissfully ignorant of it, each chapter provides some steps you and your teammates can take to make things better even without the help of the team leader. You'll be amazed how much you can do if you band together.

But what this book really promises is that you can change your team even if not another soul is in it with you. And so in each and every Toxic Team chapter there is advice to anyone who has to go it alone. If that's your reality, don't give up. I have seen many teams turn around because one determined person decided to stop wasting time and energy on a dysfunctional team. It's inspiring to watch one person choose to take the high road and to see how uncomfortable and self-conscious it makes the bad actors. Slowly, it becomes much easier for them to step up than to continue acting like children. And boy, does it feel great to be the one who said, "No more."

CHAPTER 3

The Crisis Junkie Team

In early March 2003, a 78-year-old woman boarded a flight in Guangdong Province in China en route to her home in Toronto. What she didn't know was that before she left, her lungs had been infected with a new and deadly virus: severe acute respiratory syndrome (SARS). Back in Toronto, she succumbed quickly to the disease and died quietly at her home. Tragically, before she died, she infected her son. When he got sick, he took himself to the local hospital. He, too, fell victim to the disease, but only after infecting other patients and several members of the staff. A crisis had begun.

Before public health officials really knew what was going on, grieving families and unsuspecting bystanders had spread the disease throughout the city. Carriers who didn't realize they were sick spread the virus to healthy individuals through contact at doctors' offices, church services, and even a funeral home. Even after the virus had been identified, at one hospital alone nine staff members were infected in a single day as they worked to save the life of a SARS patient.

Hospitals plunged into emergency mode. After staff members who'd followed all safety guidelines got infected, it was clear that typical protocols and standard-issue face masks wouldn't stop the highly virulent disease. Hospitals locked down. Staff members at every door filled out detailed accounts of people's movements and took everyone's temperature before allowing them into the building. I was working with three hospitals at the time and I remember going through extensive screening and sanitizing just to get into the executive offices.

Each hospital had its command center, with teams working around the clock to track and isolate the disease. Surgeries were cancelled, and friends and families were restricted from visiting loved ones—only the closest family members could be present, even for births or deaths.

Toronto was in a panic. People were wearing surgical masks on subways and airplanes. The World Health Organization recommended people avoid traveling to the city. Restaurants and theatres sat empty. Before the crisis was over, 33,000 Torontonians had been quarantined, 375 people had been infected, and 44 people had died.

Three years later, I stood in front of the executive team of one of the hospitals that had been at the epicenter of the virus. The team was discussing the SARS outbreak and how well they had performed during this defining moment. They talked about the weeks of sleepless nights and stressful, high-stakes decisions. But they also talked about their laserlike focus on what mattered—keeping their staff, patients, and community safe from further infection.

The crisis had given them something they hadn't been able to achieve for themselves. When the virus arrived, the team united around one crucial priority. Everyone knew what role they would play in solving the problem. People set aside personal conflicts and political agendas. Any resources needed were available immediately. Boring or intractable long-term issues vanished from the boardroom. Meetings shrank and focused only on updates from the staff and instructions from government public health officials. Everyone focused on the task at hand, and each person was clearly accountable for what he or she needed to get done. Those without direct responsibility were eager to help in any way possible.

The crisis allowed them to get things done. Once it was over, the team struggled to recapture that feeling. They were back to making tough decisions about which project to prioritize. They were back to stereotyped divisions between doctors and nurses, researchers and clinicians, health-care workers and accountants. Crisis was easy. Normal was hard.

Crisis Junkie team: A team that needs an urgent and immediate threat to come together and get things done.

THE VALUE OF CRISIS

It's not just in our teams. In our organizations, our governments, and our society, a crisis helps us do things that don't otherwise seem possible. Crisis gives us purpose and motivation. We love to rally and demonstrate our steely resolve when called by a higher purpose.

> You never want a serious crisis to go to waste. And what I mean by that is an opportunity to do things you think you could not do before.
> —*Rahm Emanuel, 2008*

Crisis lets us do and say things that didn't seem possible before. Somehow there is something sacred about a crisis. Who would have thought that one week before the 2012 U.S. presidential election, in the aftermath of Hurricane Sandy, Republican governor of New Jersey Chris Christie would be seen parading around with Barack Obama? But even politicians know to behave like mature, non-partisan adults in a crisis.

Think about this: We can't waste a crisis, but somehow we've come to terms with wasting all the noncrisis days we get. That's so backward!

ORIGINS OF A CRISIS JUNKIE PROBLEM

Most good teams are great in a crisis. That's not strange. It's not even a problem—it's a good thing. But a Crisis Junkie team *needs* a problem to move forward. Crisis Junkie teams lurch from crisis to crisis, only able to get work done when there's a proverbial gun to their heads. In fact, they may even create crises to feel that sense of purpose.

Why do they love the stress? Well, when the situation isn't critical, life on one of these teams is pretty demotivating. Do you recognize any of these warning signs on your team?

Lack of Role Clarity

On Crisis Junkie teams, you don't have clarity about your role and the interdependence between you and your teammates. In some cases, you have overlapping accountabilities, so you get stuck because you're afraid of stepping on toes or because you can't agree about the way forward. In other cases, gaps in accountability mean that no one feels responsible for moving an issue forward. Unclear roles are a common cause of Crisis Junkie problems.

No Clear Priorities

Crisis Junkie teams lack clear priorities. Here's one scenario: You work away at tasks, filling the days with activity that isn't really in service of anything. You're just going through the motions with no connection to why your job matters. With no real priorities, pressure, or stress, the output from your team is low. You need a crisis to shock you back to life.

Here's a more common scenario: Your team doesn't need a defibrillator to get you going—on the contrary. You're run ragged with a long list of priorities you're scrambling to accomplish. Unfortunately, this can also create a Crisis Junkie problem because it gradually takes greater and greater urgency to register on the team's Richter scale. If everything is urgent, then nothing is. The pressure keeps rising. At first, it only takes something important to get your attention, but soon you only focus on critical issues, then desperate ones, and eventually it takes a crisis before you even lift your head.

Insufficient Resources

The lack of priorities leads to another common cause of a Crisis Junkie problem: never having enough resources to do the work that needs to be done. The reason you don't have enough resources is that without priorities, you can't figure out where to spend your time and money. You can't get anything done without a crisis because you are trying to spread scarce resources across too many priorities. If you're trying to boil the ocean, you're probably not going to have enough heat. There can never be enough people, tools, or dollars to accomplish your work. So you wait for a crisis to loosen the purse strings, on one issue at least.

Politics and Infighting

Another cause of a Crisis Junkie problem is the petty squabbles and disagreements that emerge when the pressure isn't high enough on your team. I've already mentioned that Crisis Junkie teams suffer from a lack of role clarity, and that means unresolved sandbox issues often exacerbate the normal interpersonal tensions that even healthy teams have to contend with. If your teammates are constantly questioning one another, you'll never overcome the resistance to change unless there's a crisis to light a fire under everybody.

Each of these precursors makes it clear that a Crisis Junkie team is primarily, if not exclusively, a failing of your team leader. Sometimes your leader cannot, or will not, translate the organizational strategy into clear direction and priorities for your team. In other cases, your leader avoids conflict and lacks the courage to make tough decisions about what needs to be done or who gets to do what. If you have this kind of weak leader, a crisis will take the place of leadership on your team—the situation starts dictating priorities because your boss won't.

Imagine that you are on a team like this. Or maybe you don't have to imagine. You aren't sure about your role. You're trying to do way more work than is possible, especially with the limited resources you have. And every time you try to move forward, someone objects and you go back to square one. A crisis is the only thing that can clear the way for you to get something done. Maybe it's not the most important task, but at least it's something!

Fighting something (or someone) else is a welcome change from fighting one another. Using a common enemy to rally the troops is a centuries-old technique. It's a cheap, short-circuit way to create alignment, instead of doing the hard work of defining a rational, predictable purpose for the team. Unfortunately, in these situations, weak leaders learn that a crisis does the dirty work for them. Over time, they may even learn to manufacture crises as a way of aligning the team so they don't have to answer difficult questions themselves.

Crisis Junkies may look like heroes when they save the day, but wouldn't it be better to manage well enough that there weren't so many crises in the first place?

IMPACT OF BEING A CRISIS JUNKIE TEAM

At first blush, a Crisis Junkie team can look and feel like a healthy, dynamic group. Your team may even have been rewarded by superiors for "coming through" or "saving the day." There's nothing like getting an award for narrowly averting a crisis of your own making. We have got to stop reinforcing crisis management. The costs to your organization, and to you, are too high.

Crisis Junkies use the increased arousal and narrowed focus of crisis mode to get things done. For basic, even primal reasons, when we get into a crisis situation, our brains shut out extraneous detail and focus intently on the threat we're facing. When you go into crisis mode, you're less likely to access the thinking brain (the neocortex) and much more likely to rely on your animal brain. That's fine in a real life-or-death situation—there's no point in stopping to think about the cleverest way to evade a lion if the seconds spent pondering make you become its lunch.

But if you're in crisis mode at work, you'll narrow your attention to only the most critical issues, limit yourself to tasks that are required to get the job done, and censor any information that contradicts consensus or makes it more difficult to reach a decision quickly. And that means the decisions your team makes in crisis mode will be shortsighted.[1] These decisions fall into two groups:

Knee-jerk reactions. Because you're relying on your primitive brain in a crisis, the most likely thing you're going to do is rerun a scenario you've survived before. If you're working in a big retail chain and sales for the first three days of the Christmas season are disastrously low, you might reflexively slash prices and order an expensive TV ad to broadcast the sale, because that's what you did when sales slumped in 2008. But maybe this slump wasn't driven by a financial meltdown like the one in 2008. Maybe bad weather in a couple of key markets kept shoppers out of the store, and if you'd been patient, they would have come back in droves. If you let your animal brain take over and don't stop to think about what's wrong and why, you might overreact.

Risky decisions and shoddy solutions. Oversimplifying can also make you miss important information, leaving your team and your organization vulnerable. If your team doesn't take the time to think the situation through properly, something's probably going to come back to bite you later. Even if you do make the right decision, a solution created in crisis tends to be the "duct tape" version, held together by the force of will—and not much more. Anyone who has survived the airport striptease required after the Shoe Bomber or the Underwear Bomber knows that crisis solutions aren't usually sustainable.

Crisis Junkie teams also suffer from two other problems:

1. *Deteriorating relationships with other teams.* The problems aren't restricted to those inside your Crisis Junkie team.

Other teams will be infuriated by your team's inability to get things done and its habit of manufacturing faux crises. Confidence in your team will wane and your connection to the rest of the organization will be weakened. Once trust is eroded, other groups will be far less likely to collaborate with your Crisis Junkie team. Has another team in your organization ever washed its hands of dealing with you?

2. *Failure to execute strategy.* In the end, the biggest problem with Crisis Junkie teams is that they fail to execute strategy. Crises make you focus on the urgent things at the expense of the important things. Proactive, growth-oriented opportunities seldom come in the form of a crisis. Instead, the team focuses on threats. Trying to keep the worst from happening means your team misses opportunities to make sure the best *does* happen. While you're lurching from one emergency to the next, the competition is quietly using the opportunity to launch an ambitious new strategy.

Being on a Crisis Junkie team isn't just bad for your organization; it's bad for you too. Harmful effects of Crisis Junkie teams include:

Stalled career. In the short term, a crisis can be a great learning experience. In the long term, spending too much time on a Crisis Junkie team will detract from your growth and development. Crisis mode doesn't leave much time for feedback, coaching, or reflection. When things are desperate, if your finished product isn't good enough, the boss grabs it, fixes it up, and gets it out the door—without bothering to tell you what you needed to do differently. Because the next crisis is just around the corner, you never get a postmortem to learn what worked and what didn't. When your team is perpetually in crisis mode, you don't get a proper chance to learn.

Stress and burnout. Repeated crises take a huge toll on you. The urgency of the situation, whether warranted or not, forces you to go to heroic lengths to avoid catastrophe. This means late nights, skipped meals, interrupted sleep, and a whole host of other unsustainable behavior. And if you're on a Crisis Junkie team, I won't even ask about the last time you made it to the gym. Not only is this stress bad for you; it's also terrible for your family and friends, who suffer the fallout when the scales of your work-life balance tip too far toward the office.

DIAGNOSTIC

Your team won't just wake up one morning with an extreme Crisis Junkie problem. The early signs of a problem might surface long before the effects become critical. Use the simple diagnostic test in Figure 3.1 to see the level of risk on your team. If you want to use this test with your teammates, it, along with the other tools from this book, is available at www.ChangeYourTeam.com.

Symptoms		True
Early Warning	People on my team struggle with lack of role clarity.	☐
	We have far more priorities than it's possible to deliver on.	☐
	We are more likely to work on urgent tasks than important ones.	☐
	We find excuses for why things can't be done.	☐
	We "duck" and avoid working on initiatives unless forced.	☐
Moderate Case	We perform significantly better under stress and with deadlines.	☐
	Important action items get "lost between the cracks" and not completed.	☐
	We fail to learn from past crises and seldom look back on what happened.	☐
	We spend significant effort on politics and image management.	☐
	We will fix things only after they get to the breaking point.	☐
Severe Case	My team leader uses crises outside the team to bring us together.	☐
	We reward and celebrate heroics rather than good planning.	☐
	Issues are artificially inflated to increase the urgency of the response.	☐
	We are unable to make decisions unless forced.	☐
	We ignore contrary information or anything that would slow us down.	☐
	Total	—

Figure 3.1 Crisis Junkie Team Diagnostic Test

If you found that only one or two of the early warning signs apply, you're in good shape. No need to worry about a Crisis Junkie problem taking hold on your team. If your team has four or more of these symptoms, you need to get serious about your looming Crisis Junkie problem.

Triage and Emergency Medicine

You can take steps to reduce the negative impacts of your Crisis Junkie team. Truly fixing a Crisis Junkie problem will take considerable time and investment, but the following suggestions will stem the bleeding long enough to tackle the issue more systematically.

As you read these lists, you might shudder to think about attempting any of these techniques directly with your boss. After all, team leaders are often the ones responsible for a Crisis Junkie problem. Don't give up before you try. Give your boss the benefit of the doubt. Maybe she wants out of the crisis habit. Maybe she can learn. If you don't try, you're contributing to the problem.

If you're lucky, when you put this book on your team leader's desk with a bookmark in this chapter, she'll own up to the issue and say she's ready to do something about it. And if you are a team leader, you are in a great position to change your team for the better.

If you are the team leader or if your team leader is on board:

1. *Define your team mandate.* One of the reasons you get trapped in crisis mode is a lack of clarity about what the team is supposed to be doing. You need to go back to square one and define the purpose of the team. What is the organization counting on you to do? How will your team move the organization forward, instead of just ensuring it doesn't slip backward? This mandate will help you add some proactive items to your agenda.

2. *Fix your meetings.* Based on your mandate, take a look at how you're spending your time together. Do you have room

for the right discussions and decisions? Can you add standing agenda items to make sure the important stuff doesn't lose out to the urgent stuff? Can you use ad hoc meetings to deal with urgent matters so that there is still time in standing meetings to address the forward agenda?

This is what the hospital executive team from the SARS story did. They got clear about what they needed to work on as a team and also what they needed to leave for individuals outside the team to do. Giving individuals more autonomy allowed them to get a lot more done without getting into arguments—even without a crisis to bring them together. When they came together as a team, it was to work on issues they needed to solve together, and everyone knew what they needed to accomplish.

Now, if you try to engage your team leader and it doesn't work, it's no excuse to give up. If your team leader isn't on board, but your teammates are willing to make things better, there's a lot you can do to make real progress. If you have siblings, think of how much you could accomplish when you were in cahoots—your parents didn't stand a chance!

If your teammates are on board:

1. *Work on role clarity.* You might assume that without the support of your boss, you can't improve role clarity. That's nonsense. As long as the team agrees about who is doing what, any misdirection of work from the team leader can be corrected among the team. If the team leader gives you work with murky boundaries and unclear accountabilities, huddle up and figure it out. Approach your teammate: *"I know Sarah assigned this to me, but I think this is more appropriate for you. Does that make sense? How can I help?"*

2. *Get issues resolved.* If you're in this pickle, you and your teammates do bear some responsibility. Your boss probably uses crises because she can't get you to agree without one.

Time to start agreeing how you'll make decisions when you disagree. Start with one issue that has been a sore spot, agree first *how* you will reach agreement (i.e., what are the criteria you will use), and then apply the criteria and make the decision. If you and your teammates can act like grownups, your boss won't need to resort to childish tactics to get you to work together.

If your team leader isn't ready to check into Crisis Junkie rehab and your teammates are content with petty squabbling, you're going to have to make things better yourself. Granted, you won't be able to solve the whole problem, but that's no reason not to make things better where you can.

When you are going it alone:

1. *Learn from the past.* Pick one recent crisis and analyze it. What events led up to the crisis? What could you have done to avoid it, to give the team more time to deal with it, or to improve the quality of decisions made while in it? Your team probably has a pattern and if you figure it out, you'll be better prepared the next time sales plummet, the system crashes, or a hurricane knocks out power.

   What data could you monitor to get earlier warnings about issues? What information could you keep at hand to help improve decision making when the crisis hits? Could you use stakeholders outside the team to influence the team leader to be responsive even without a crisis? There are things you can do to reduce the frequency of crises and improve their outcomes when they happen.

2. *Reduce the impact.* Last, if you are not going to be able make much of a dent in the Crisis Junkie problem on your team, you can at least reduce the dent it makes in you. Get disciplined about staying on top of things in the quiet periods. Use the calm before the storm to deal with issues so you can focus on the crisis without getting so underwater

on everything else. Then find a stress-management strategy that works for you and *do not stop* when the crisis comes. Exercise, 10-minute time-outs every couple of hours, meditation, mindfulness—find what works for you to stay just a little removed from the fray. If this is going to be your reality, you need to adapt.

None of these techniques on its own will make a truly toxic Crisis Junkie team healthy. But they will make it better. And making progress with one technique will build your confidence and your credibility when you try another.

If you've been living a frustrating existence slogging away and getting nowhere, and then suddenly you experience the exhilaration of coming through in a crisis, it's easy to see why you might get hooked. But an addiction to crisis is just as dangerous as any other addiction. If your team is jonesing for the next crisis, it's time to sober up.

CHAPTER 4

The Bobble Head Team

A large multinational real estate company owned and managed industrial spaces and shopping malls. Most members of the executive team had been together for several years. It was the kind of organization where people could rise through the ranks all the way from the front lines to the executive suite. Everyone was proud of their great track record of promoting from within.

Their long history together made it easy for the team to communicate. Every member knew the organization inside and out. In their time climbing the corporate ladder, most had visited different business units and had performed different functions. Some had even worked on assignments in their international locations. It took me a few meetings to understand their special shorthand lingo.

Everything on the team was very pleasant. When they gathered for meetings, they'd chat about the weekend or the kids' sports tournaments, because most of them knew one another's families. When it came to talking shop, they knew one another's direct reports and could relate to the successes and challenges that they faced.

For the very rare person who came in from the outside, it took a long time to be seen as one of the team. I remember in my first conversation with the head of marketing, he made an offhand remark about being the new guy.

"Oh really," I said. "How long have you been here?"

"Only 8 years," he said. It was all the more ridiculous because his previous job was as the account manager for the company at their public relations agency. He'd actually been working with the organization for two decades.

In early 2008, the board started to make noise about their competitive position. They'd grown over the past 10 years, but the competition had grown faster. Real estate companies that had been roughly the same size as theirs in 1998 were now two and three times their size. They decided they couldn't accept this relative underperformance.

They set up a task force to come up with ways to close the gap. The task force said it was time to stop playing it safe and to start entering some more lucrative, but riskier, lines of business. They wanted to change their product mix to take advantage of the red-hot corporate real estate market. They'd need to recruit new, bigger investors. And they'd need to expand into new markets, to capitalize on growth in the developing world. Sure, business worked differently in those places, but it was a huge opportunity.

Discussions went smoothly because they all liked and trusted one another. After only four executive team meetings, they made their decision: They would launch a new business line and invest significant resources to get it up to speed quickly. It was a big bet, but it was the only way to close the gap with the competition.

Fast-forward to the fall of 2008. Lehman Brothers was bankrupt. Major financial players needed U.S. government bailouts. Construction, both residential and corporate, ground to a halt. Vacancy rates at office towers were the highest they'd been in decades. But for this team, the meltdown came just in time. They'd made their plans and had even started to hire people for the new business line, but they hadn't quite pulled the trigger yet. The meltdown saved them from a risky, shortsighted plan. They were about to jump into a crashing market. They would have spent the reserves that were now helping them ride out the effects of the recession on their core business. It was a very close call.

How did they come so close to the edge?

The team had become its own worst enemy. They had lost sight of the value of diversity of thought and the importance of conflict in arriving at good decisions. Things felt good on the team, and everyone wanted to keep it that way.

The team leader didn't help, either. His strong, controlling personality made it difficult to disagree with him. If you tried to disagree, he would rephrase what you said to make it sound like you agreed with him. If you did it too many times, you might find yourself out of a job.

Shortly after the crisis, they brought me in to guide them through a team session using a personality assessment. When I opened up the team report, I quickly saw that most of the team was clustered in one corner of the grid of personality types. Five of the 16 possible cells—a whole section of the grid—were empty. And they weren't just missing random types: The empty cells were the ones that were most different from the CEO's style.

I pointed this out when I presented the results to the team. "Looks like you've culled the herd," I said.

There was a moment's silence and then, with a sly smile, the CEO chimed in. "Oh good," he said. "It's working."

A day after the meeting, my assistant handed me a fax. On the single sheet was a photocopy of a grid, with people's initials written in. The date at the top showed me that it was the executive team, four years earlier. I noticed two things. First, people were distributed much more evenly across the grid. Second, the names in the now empty boxes belonged to four members of the executive team who had left the company. I was right: They had culled the herd.

The picture was becoming clear. The team was very comfortable together. Under the direction of a strong leader, they had become aligned. Those who didn't share the same worldview had either been fired or had left out of frustration. Faced with a very big decision about a risky new strategy, under strong pressure from the board, they had overestimated their capabilities, underplayed the risk, and smiled their way to significant peril. I was looking at a Bobble Head team.

Bobble Head Team: A team that is too aligned and doesn't have enough diversity or dissent to make good decisions.

THE DESIRE FOR HARMONY

Human beings need to belong. We need to feel connected to those around us, to feel wanted and needed by our peers. That need allows us to cooperate—in collecting food, or protecting against predators, or building a railroad, or designing and manufacturing a shiny new gadget. Belonging, harmony, and community are absolutely necessary for success.

But sometimes we let that desire to belong go too far. Remember when you were 14? Did you ever do something silly in a desperate attempt to fit in? Did you ever memorize the lyrics to Led Zeppelin (or Elvis, or U2) to impress someone like I did? Did you do reckless things that you're lucky to have survived? The desire to fit in can easily become the pressure to conform.

Unfortunately, these pressures don't magically disappear when you're an adult. When you join a team, you naturally want to connect with the members, to feel liked, and to be valued for your contribution. That's a good thing, because it supports group cohesiveness, which is the glue that keeps your team together. But when the need to belong gets too strong, you start agreeing with everyone just to feel like one of the team.

It's a precarious balance. We need connectedness and harmony to form healthy teams. And yet we're desperately vulnerable to letting that cohesiveness go too far. When you're too motivated to say "yes," you can lose sight of what you're saying yes to. So you have the difficult task of disrupting harmony just enough to be productive, but not so much that you destroy the connectedness of the group.

ORIGINS OF A BOBBLE HEAD PROBLEM

Now, don't get me wrong. It's really important that groups come together and align around a common goal. Indeed, that's the first step in forming a team. But a Bobble Head team has *uniformity* instead of alignment. When you're on a Bobble Head team, you don't just align on where you're going; you stay in lockstep every inch of the way. You are so together that you can't see when you are putting yourselves at risk. You nod your head all the time because it feels good when you do.

Have you ever noticed that one of the following factors makes it easier to agree than to disagree on your team?

Familiarity

When discussing our reactions to classical music, my high school music teacher used to say, "You don't know what you like, you like what you know." And so it is with most things for us humans—we like the familiar. The more your team gets to know one another, the more comfortable you are with one another's quirks. You even get used to bad habits, and you stop noticing your teammates' indiscretions. When I work with a team for the first time, I'll call out bad behavior that everyone else seems not to notice. *"Oh, yeah, that's just Bob,"* people will say. *"He does that."* Do you know your teammates so well that you can finish one another's sentences? Familiarity makes you more likely to go with the flow.

Homogeneity

If your team consists of people who are very similar to one another, that also makes you vulnerable to the Bobble Head plague. Healthy teams need diversity. Diversity doesn't just mean gender balance, racial or cultural representation, or international membership. It's true that having team members of different nationalities, cultures, or genders is likely to strengthen your team. But diversity goes well beyond visible differences. Even if you're on a very multicultural team, you can become Bobble Heads because your team members are identical in other ways: You've worked in the same organization your whole careers; you're all engineers, or bankers, or doctors; you all come from the same socioeconomic group and went to the same prestigious universities. Your team doesn't have to look alike to become a Bobble Head team—you just have to think alike.

Overbearing Team Leader

Controlling team leaders also encourage Bobble Head–ism. Some of these leaders control you outright by telling you what is and is not acceptable. Others are more subtle, signaling what's acceptable and unacceptable by giving or withholding their attention. If every time you agree with your boss you get praised, and every time you disagree you get chastised or ignored, you'll learn pretty quickly to stifle disagreement. Eventually you won't even realize you're suppressing your opposition. At that point, you aren't thinking about the benefit of agreeing or disagreeing, you're starting to just agree by default. Once you accept the team's opinion as your own, you have become a Bobble Head.

High Stress

The pressure to conform doesn't always come from inside your team. Strong pressure from outside your team can also create Bobble Heads. Faced with a threat from outside the team, it's natural to rally together. You might be aware of having intentionally tried to reduce dissent and focus on the enemy outside of the team. Benjamin Franklin used that technique beautifully in his famous quote during the signing of the Declaration of Independence:

> We must all hang together, or assuredly we shall all hang separately.

If you're anxious enough about the risk outside the team, you might not even be aware that you're suppressing your disagreement. But whether you are conscious of it or not, the more pressure your team is under from the outside, the more likely you are to stop challenging and start agreeing.

IMPACT OF BEING A BOBBLE HEAD TEAM

Being a part of a Bobble Head team can feel pretty good. The mood is pleasant. The conversation is supportive and empathetic. In its most innocuous form, a Bobble Head team just goes with the flow and turns out run-of-the-mill work.

Unfortunately, vanilla, passable work is about the *best* you can hope for from a Bobble Head team. Once the desire for harmony outweighs the desire to make a good decision, and the team starts to slide toward groupthink, the costs become more extreme. You and your teammates might convince yourselves that your plan for safety in your factories is good enough, but what if it's not? What if you've ignored a critical emergency scenario? You might create a plan to deal with a new competitor entering the market, but is it sufficient? What if you're overconfident about your position? What if you're kidding yourselves?

Poor decisions. Bobble Head team discussions lack the balance that one or two devil's advocates would provide. The most immediate result is that you fail to collect enough information during the decision-making process. Without at least one voice chiming in with *"What about . . . ,"* you're likely to stick to the most obvious and readily available information. You're making decisions based on limited facts played out over relatively few scenarios. You've got blinders on. And that means you're not seeing risk.

False confidence. Once you've made a decision, the next problem on your Bobble Head team is overconfidence in your ability to execute the plan. Because you've glossed over important facts in your rush to agree, your plans and budgets may be wildly optimistic. This is what happened to the real estate company at the beginning of the chapter. Do you relate? Has your team ever created an overly optimistic plan and promised great success (additional revenue, new customers, cost savings) based on a cursory evaluation of the environment? Did you invest significant resources to achieve these fabulous things, only to realize it wasn't going to work after it was too late to turn back? Has your team ever watched a pipe dream go up in smoke?

Formation of "us" and "them." To maintain your Bobble Head team's false sense of the world, you often need to protect against dissenting views from other teams. This can lead to an adversarial dynamic among teams in your organization, which destroys collaboration. In fact, the leaders in your organization will probably notice a problem brewing *among* teams before they notice the problem *within* your Bobble Head team itself, where everyone seems to be getting along so well.

As a member of a Bobble Head team, you'll probably feel very comfortable for a while. Life can feel pretty relaxing on cruise control, but eventually you will suffer from the personal effects of being on a Bobble Head team, too.

Loss of self. I once learned that children in a choir often sing slightly off key so that they can hear their own voice. When they match their pitch to the choir, their voice disappears into the mass. Being on a Bobble Head team is like being in perfect tune with the choir all the time—you begin to lose your own voice. After a while, you begin to question what value you bring. And you'll find it hard to advance your career, because you won't be able to point to many distinct accomplishments or to the unique value that you brought to the team.

Risk of blame. When things go wrong on a Bobble Head team, somebody has to take the blame. If you could have and should have prevented a poor decision from being made, your reputation will suffer. If you have never gone on record with possible issues or concerns, you are vulnerable to becoming a scapegoat—particularly if your boss is quick to deflect the oncoming bullets.

DIAGNOSTIC

It can be tough to tell if you're on a Bobble Head team, because all teams do need some group cohesiveness to be effective. Use the diagnostic test in Figure 4.1 to find out if your team is sailing happily into the sunset or if you're heading for a cliff.

TRIAGE AND EMERGENCY MEDICINE

Scores of two or three symptoms from the early warning symptoms of the quiz suggest that you are keeping your team open to different perspectives. If your score is higher than four, you are headed for a Bobble Head problem. It's important to start working on it right away. One person can significantly improve a Bobble Head team. It just takes some courage and a willingness to speak up.

As in the previous chapter, think about which members of your team might be open to working on the problem. Depending on who is willing to try, you'll have different solutions at your disposal. Assume the best-case scenario first.

Symptoms		True
Early Warning	People on my team have worked together for a long time.	☐
	We have similar backgrounds in terms of training and education.	☐
	We have a strong team leader with whom we tend to agree.	☐
	We spend significantly more time together than with others outside.	☐
	We value our positive group relations.	☐
Moderate Case	We tend to embrace ideas enthusiastically.	☐
	Our decision-making process is focused and quick.	☐
	We downplay the importance of negative or disconfirming information.	☐
	We defer to the team leader, even when we might disagree.	☐
	We have a track record of overpromising and underdelivering.	☐
Severe Case	It has been a long time since a team member disagreed openly.	☐
	We actively exclude information that contradicts our point of view.	☐
	Our consensus leads us to riskier and riskier decisions.	☐
	We criticize and shut out other teams who don't go along with our plans.	☐
	There have been significant consequences of our poor decision making.	☐
	Total	——

Figure 4.1   Bobble Head Team Diagnostic Test

If you are the team leader or your team leader is on board:

1. *Formalize the decision-making process.* One of the biggest problems on a Bobble Head team is that decisions are based on insufficient information or biased reviews of the information that is available. With your team leader's help, you

can introduce a formal decision-making model that describes the steps in decision making, the criteria you will use to make decisions, the breadth of data and opinions you will consider, and even the roles that team members will be expected to play to increase the diversity of thought. Documenting your decision process will help you to stick to a consistent, thorough process, even when it's uncomfortable.

2. *Involve external stakeholders.* Another very effective way to reduce your team's Bobble Head tendencies is to invite external stakeholders to join your meetings. By introducing new people, you'll shed light on otherwise overlooked perspectives. When you bring these people in, let them know what you're looking for. Tell them that you're concerned you are "breathing your own fumes," as one of my clients puts it. If you specifically ask them to share contrary opinions, they'll be more comfortable speaking up.

Given that one of the factors that contributes to a Bobble Head team is a controlling boss, it might be overly optimistic to think you'll have his buy-in. Not to worry. As with any Toxic Team, the members of a Bobble Head team can meaningfully improve it even without the boss's cooperation.

If your teammates are on board:

1. *Rotate roles.* It's hard for one person to always be the naysayer. If you are usually the customer advocate, or the financially prudent one, you probably get ignored because you're always saying the same things. Have you given up even trying? Instead of shouldering the burden yourself, take turns with teammates playing different roles to make sure the message gets heard. If you and your teammates each have a responsibility to represent an issue or a

stakeholder, you won't give in as easily. You won't want to let the team down by neglecting your job.

2. *Disagree nicely.* If your team is tight-knit and wants to keep it that way, find ways to introduce dissenting views in a way that feels positive and supportive. This topic is the entire focus of Chapter 13, but to tide you over, here are a couple of important points. First, show your teammates that you value different opinions. Simple phrases like, *"I hadn't thought of it from that perspective,"* or *"Interesting, I didn't know that"* make it obvious that you can disagree and still like and value one another. Second, respond to disagreement with questions that show your interest and openness: *"What should we do with that new information?" "How will that impact the plan we were working on?"* You'll protect the diversity of thought without compromising on group harmony.

The real estate team at the beginning of the chapter changed when the team members got serious about introducing more healthy debate. The team leader wasn't really comfortable with it, but that didn't deter the members from speaking up. When the leader dismissed one person's comments, someone else would step up and echo their concerns. Eventually, the team got comfortable kicking the tires and the leader realized the debate helped them spot risks.

If your team leader is still expecting his yes men and yes women to nod along and your teammates are too content to notice there's a problem, then it's up to you to reduce the risk of bad decisions.

When you are going it alone:

1. *Appoint yourself devil's advocate.* A great devil's advocate can help a team make better decisions. First, focus on the quality of evidence being presented. If it's shoddy, suggest some

ways it could be improved. For example, *"The data from that pilot project do look promising in that small district in the Northeast. How do we think the program will land with our customers on the West Coast?"* Second, offer alternate conclusions based on the same data: *"I think it's possible that the increase in sales is more a result of the improving economy rather than our new ad campaign."* Last, avoid the temptation to question your individual teammates. Once it's personal, you're threatening group harmony and you risk being rejected. Stick to the facts.

2. *Find connections outside the team.* Because a Bobble Head problem stems from the basic human need to belong, it will be hard for you to resist if your teammates are the only people you talk to. To strengthen your resolve, find other groups at work to connect with. It could be people with your technical expertise from across different departments. It could be people who all go to the same gym after work. The nature of the group isn't important. Just find an outlet so that you don't depend on your teammates to feel valued and connected.

A Bobble Head team can be a welcome relief if you've endured nasty, vindictive groups in the past. But don't get too comfortable with all that harmony. Your team and your organization are counting on you to make sure the team makes sound decisions. Stop nodding and start being deliberate about when to agree and when to offer a different perspective.

CHAPTER 5

The Spectator Team

I sat quietly in the boardroom, my chair pushed up against the wall so I could watch without interfering with the action. The team took their seats around the table. I'd started working with this team about eight months before. At that time, their biggest issue was that they had no confidence in one another. They routinely invaded one another's territory because they didn't believe their colleagues could handle the work.

It took several months, but they turned the team around. They learned to listen without jumping to conclusions. They even made rules for how they would fight with one another so they'd be comfortable with healthy debate. The tone of their discussions improved. The team was enjoying the feeling of being successful again.

This was my first time observing them in a regular team meeting. They started right on time. Everybody had a role: a timekeeper, a note taker, and the team leader, who as the meeting chair was keeping everything neat and tidy. They raised the first item of business, the project owner presented it to the team, everyone nodded, and the matter was closed. It didn't even take five minutes.

This pattern continued, with the team leader periodically glancing over at me as if to say *"See, look how well we're doing!"* Each time, the person presenting would pass out some material and speak for 5 or 10 minutes to review the highlights of the information. The team leader would then ask a few questions, which the presenter would answer without input from the rest of the team. And the other five pairs of eyes would bounce back and forth as though we were at a tennis match.

The pendulum had swung too far the other way. Instead of everybody trying to do everybody else's work for them, now everybody was leaving everybody else completely alone. Every idea left the meeting in exactly the same form it entered. Which means, of course, there was no reason to have the meeting at all!

The team leader was a big part of the problem. In his efforts to run a tight ship, he'd packed 13 items onto the agenda for a two-hour meeting. I couldn't help but remember that classic scene from *I Love Lucy* where Lucille Ball is working in the chocolate factory. She can't keep up with her job of wrapping the sweets so she shoves more and more chocolates into her mouth as the conveyor belt moves faster and faster. These team members were just trying to keep up with the volume of information being shoved down their throats. They definitely didn't have time to digest what anyone was saying.

This method worked well for simple things like updating everyone on the budget. But then the human resources person was given 10 minutes to present on building a high-performance culture. The thought that (a) you could cover transforming the culture in 10 minutes, and that (b) the human resources person could drive culture change without the rest of the team, was totally ridiculous. I couldn't stay quiet any longer. I popped up from the back row to ask, "How do you guys want to handle this issue?" Finally the team snapped out of their trance and asked for a specific meeting just to discuss the culture issue. Phew!

This was another Toxic Team. This time, the problem was the silent killer—the Spectator team. These teams aren't teams at all; they're just a bunch of individuals coming together to hear each other talk about their portfolios. My seven-year-old would call it show and tell: Each member brings their favorite toy and shares it in hopes of impressing the other kids. But no one really cares about anyone else's stuff. And they certainly don't add any value beyond their own portfolio. *They just show up, report in, and tune out.*

Spectator Team: A team where the whole is equal to the sum of the parts because individual members contribute only in their own areas, with little discussion or debate.

OVERLOAD

We are overloaded. Before 2008, we were running too fast, doing too much. After 2008, we're doing the same but with fewer people. Most people I know live in a constant state of panic. I'm no different. I shoo my kids out the door in the morning, saying, "I'm gonna be late. Go! Go! Go!" as though my 7- and 11-year-old daughters were training for *The Amazing Race*. I run down the subway stairs in pumps, risking a broken ankle, as if I can't afford to miss a train and wait 90 whole seconds for the next one. I'm often in four different meetings before noon, no time for even a cup of tea or a bathroom break in between. I fly out the door at 5:25, cutting it close to get the kids to dancing or piano in time. Sometimes teammates walk with me to the elevator, just to find the time for one last urgent item. I log back in once the kids are in bed and desperately try to get my inbox back to zero before starting the evening's tasks.

In my crazy world, there is no one I value more than a teammate who is on top of her game. Sometimes the person really is very capable—so I'm confident that if they have done something, they've done it well. Sometimes it's a person with different technical expertise than me. I don't have the time or energy to get up to speed on their subject matter—so I just assume it's good. Other times it's just about the volume of work. I haven't read a document that was distributed in advance, so I sit back and leave the discussion to the people who did. There are so many seemingly innocent ways that we check out from our teams.

When you don't need to pay attention to your teammates' projects, you can use your energy on your own to-do list. And that's what your team is counting on you for, right? To do your work really,

really well. *That's the trap.* You forget that your team needs your attention and energy not just on your own work, but on the team's work.

The minute you give in to the temptation to relax, sit back, and just watch your teammates in action, you become a spectator. And a Spectator team isn't a team at all; it's just a group of people who occasionally sit in the same room.

Origins of a Spectator Team

As with each of the Toxic Teams, the Spectator team develops without anyone really noticing that something is going wrong. You let one comment slide and nothing bad happens. Then all of a sudden you're off in daydream land. How many of these precursors to a Spectator problem can you see on your team?

No Team Mandate

Does your team spend hundreds of hours together for no clear purpose? If you're on a Spectator team, your team leader probably *thinks* you have a clear reason for getting together, but those descriptions are usually just the sum of the parts. *"Bob takes care of our confectionary sales team, Mandi is responsible for our cookie business, Latisha looks after cakes."* That's nice, but what do they need to do together? Without a clear purpose for bringing the team together (such as how to improve the relationship with a big grocery chain, in this example), your team is relegated to fourth-grade book report territory—listening to Bob rave on about the new formulation for gum that changes color when you chew it, and Latisha get all excited about green cake batter for St. Patrick's Day. No wonder you zone out!

Technical Expertise Overvalued

Some Spectator teams assume you need deep technical expertise in a subject to add value. This might be a big problem for you if you're on a cross-functional team where your team members have very different roles. Do you hesitate to weigh in on an issue because you don't know as much as the person talking? Does your team fail to appreciate the powerful impact of a good naïve question? If one person on your team is considered *the source* on a particular issue, the rest of you probably aren't contributing much.

Different Capability

I'm working right now with a team that gathers people with very different skill levels around one table. You can really tell who was on the debating team in high school—and who's not comfortable speaking off the cuff. Some of the members are charismatic, persuasive, and quick on their feet. Others can't really hold their own when things heat up. It's like a sporting event with professional players and amateurs on the field together. The pros will inadvertently injure the amateurs. They don't mean to, but capable, ambitious people tend to go hard and the quality of the game relies on everyone being able to engage with the same intensity. Those members of the team who can't keep up stick to the safety of the benches. They become spectators.

Maybe you're a spectator because you and your teammates have an unspoken pact: *"Don't make my idea look bad in front of the boss and I won't make yours look bad, either."* If so, you're probably reacting to a particularly nasty boss. But if you've gone beyond not throwing one another under the bus and have started to resent anyone who makes a suggestion, you're in trouble. That's when instead of sharing ideas and contributing to the discussion, you just clam up and wait for your turn to present.

IMPACT OF BEING A SPECTATOR TEAM

Spectator teams can feel productive and efficient. The team leader from the beginning of this chapter sure thought so. He was just cruising along, wasting no time on chitchat. Of course, part of the purpose of having a team is the chitchat, or at least the interchange of ideas. Without strong, healthy debate, your team is missing out on all the amazing value that teams provide. Here are some of the repercussions of a Spectator team.

Wasted time. Spectator teams waste a lot of time in unproductive meetings. How many hours a year does your team spend in meetings? Many spend at least 100 hours together per year. If ideas leave the meeting room in exactly the same form as they entered, you've made the time in the middle pretty much useless. So you're talking about *weeks* of wasted time and the equivalent of tens of thousands of dollars of lost productivity. Can your organization afford that?

Siloed thinking. Work that's done by an individual on your team without input from other members is likely to be one-dimensional. Without the benefit of complementary expertise, unique perspectives, and different styles, the work just isn't as strong as it could be. The finance recommendation lacks the insight about how suppliers will react. The operations plan doesn't consider the impact of process changes on customers or on the brand. The world is too competitive and too dynamic for one-dimensional solutions—they won't hold up under pressure.

Implementation struggles. Although you feel like speed demons during the decision-making process, your Spectator team tends to turn into slowpokes when you start trying to implement a plan. Members of your team have only gotten a superficial sense of the issues and haven't thought through all the implications of the plan. Those stakeholder groups you ignored while planning suddenly get wind of what's going on and want to have a say. Even people who were in the room when the decision was made start to appreciate the plan in new ways. And then you're back to the drawing board.

For you as an individual, the impact of being on a Spectator team takes a while to notice. It's not like some of the other Toxic Teams, which are uncomfortable in the moment. A Spectator team can feel alright, for a while. But being a member of a Spectator team has its downside.

Disengagement. You may have become a Spectator to cope with overwork, but eventually it's going to make it harder and harder for you to get anything done. You feel connected to something when you're a meaningful part of it. The more you withdraw from the conversation, the less you can take pride in your contribution. Slowly but surely, you contribute less and less. You start leaving meetings early, once your agenda item has been covered. You miss the odd meeting, assuming no one will mind. At some point, no one on the team can count on you to really show up, whether you're in the room or not. You've made yourself irrelevant. When you really do have something to add, no one gives you the time of day. And unfortunately, that probably feels worse for you than it does for your teammates.

DIAGNOSTIC

If you have trust and confidence in your teammates and you don't chime in on every single issue that comes up, there's no need to call 911. But if your name hasn't shown up in the meeting minutes since 2010, you might start to get worried. Use the quick diagnostic test in Figure 5.1 to see if a Spectator problem might be brewing on your team.

	Symptoms	True
Early Warning	We usually talk only when agenda items are directly relevant to us.	☐
	We primarily use meetings to share information.	☐
	There is little discussion and debate in our meetings.	☐
	Team members seldom seek input on issues outside meetings.	☐
	We keep our discussions very focused.	☐
Moderate Case	People spend lots of time in meetings responding to e-mails.	☐
	Most conversations are between a single team member and the boss.	☐
	We tend to forget what we've covered because we don't really listen.	☐
	People present fully formed ideas for the team's approval.	☐
	My team leader keeps discussion on items to a minimum.	☐
Severe Case	My teammates get very upset if someone critiques their ideas.	☐
	My team leader dominates every discussion.	☐
	My teammates have become disengaged.	☐
	We often miss stakeholders that should have been considered.	☐
	Debate happens after a decision is made, during implementation.	☐
	Total	—

Figure 5.1   Spectator Team Diagnostic Test

TRIAGE AND EMERGENCY MEDICINE

If the scores suggest you are at risk for a Spectator problem, it's time to re-engage. It shouldn't be too difficult to start contributing more.

First, figure out who else is on your side. The following tactics are divided up based on who wants to get on the field and who's content to stay on the sidelines. As always, let's think positively first.

If you are the team leader or your team leader is on board:

1. *Develop a team mandate.* A team mandate is a statement that describes the value of your team to your organization. It should explain what the team is responsible for doing together and why the team meets. Don't include anything that an individual team member can handle without the group's input. Instead, focus on the interdependencies and places where your individual accountabilities overlap. In a sales team, the purpose of the team might be to develop the optimum sales tools by drawing on aspects of each salesperson's technique. In a human resources team, it might be to support a new productivity strategy through changes in recruiting, training, organization structure, and compensation. The important thing is that the mandate describes a purpose for the team that draws on everyone's expertise.

2. *Reset your meetings and agendas.* Once you have defined the team's purpose, re-evaluate the content of your meetings, looking for things that can be removed and other things that need to be added. Find other ways to share individual team member updates or at least make them no more than 20 percent of the agenda. That will leave room for topics you've been neglecting. Many of these topics are the strategic issues you've shoved out of the way to cover urgent issues within individual team members' portfolios. A revamped agenda will be a much-needed injection of energy into a team that is accustomed to talking about things that should be handled elsewhere.

Not every team leader is ready to give up the relative calm and good order of their Spectator team. That's okay; maybe your teammates have had enough of playing Angry Birds under the table.

If your teammates are on board:

1. *Change the code.* If your team has followed an unwritten rule of never commenting on one another's topics, talk about how you can help one another more. After a painful implementation process, talk about what wasn't discussed during decision making that might have made things go more smoothly. Did you miss some key issues? Did you neglect a particular point of view? If so, talk about how to raise these perspectives during decision making. *"We missed the boat on the implementation plan on the Goldwater Mining project. How are we going to get the implementation issues on the table during planning next time?"* Assign roles to different team members by asking one person to think through the implications for your suppliers, or choose another person to focus specifically on budget issues. People with specific roles to play will be less likely to sit back during team discussions.

2. *Seek input before the meeting.* If meeting time is precious and your boss is obsessed with sticking to an ambitious agenda, your team needs to find other opportunities to help one another. Try sending around materials before the meeting and convening a casual meeting with some of your teammates in advance. You'll quickly learn who your go-to teammates are on different topics. When you actively seek out their help, you'll wake them up a little. It'll be easier for them to disagree with you when the boss isn't in the room. True, you're inviting constructive criticism when you could have just sailed through. But it's worth it: You'll find you'll save time and be more successful implementing a plan when you take the time to build it thoughtfully.

It is possible, unfortunately, that you will be the only person on your team who isn't content to use team meetings to clean out their inboxes or catch up on lost sleep. That is no reason to give in. One less Spectator is one less Spectator. Put down your popcorn and get in the game. Here are two ways to start:

1. *Ask great questions.*   It can be a shock to the system to go from checked-out to full-on active participant all at once. Bridge this gap by starting to ask more questions. When your teammates present their ideas, highlight issues they've missed with general open-ended questions like, *"What would Manufacturing think of this?"* Prompt other members of the team to get involved, too: *"Deidre, how do you think your folks will react?"* Slowly, you'll bring one or two people back from the bleachers and re-engage them in the discussion.

2. *Connect outside the meeting.*   If the passive culture of your team is so strong that your attempts to add value in the meeting keep failing, you are going to have to find another outlet. During your meetings, take good notes on your own questions, ideas, and concerns. Then, when things are quiet, get together with your teammates to share your ideas. *"Your project on reducing water usage in our plants is really exciting. I had a few ideas while you were talking. Do you have time for a coffee?"* Your teammates should appreciate the input as long as you project genuine enthusiasm or concern for their success.

When you are overwhelmed by your workload, it's tempting to find places to conserve energy. If your teammates seem to have it covered, why not just stay focused on your own work? Well, because your contribution to your teammates' work is just as critical as your own work. If it weren't, you could just disband the team right now. Teams are supposed to be greater than the sum of their parts. It's the contributions you make on everyone else's ideas, and those that they make on yours, that create that great multiplier effect. It's time to get it working for your team.

CHAPTER 6

The Bleeding Back Team

When I stepped off the elevator for my first in-person session with a particular finance management team, I immediately understood the origin of the expression "working at the top of the house." I was so high up I had to repressurize my ears. I must admit that I was a little awestruck by the surroundings: the massive foyer, the wood-paneled elevator doors, the exquisite art on the walls. Everything on this executive floor signaled that decorum was the order of the day. I hid my ratty old briefcase in a cupboard in the meeting room and quickly put on some lipstick.

Slowly, the members of the team arrived. They were impeccably dressed and had firm corporate handshakes. After introducing themselves, they found their spots at the massive oak table, poured themselves coffee in china cups, and proceeded to make polite small talk with one another.

If you had looked in through a window, these folks would have looked like a friendly, healthy, cooperative team. The discussion was perfectly polite. Nobody raised their voices. Almost everyone participated. They even laughed occasionally. You would have thought I could pack my bags and move on to a team who actually needed my help. And you would have been very wrong.

The scene playing out in the room was nothing more than a well-rehearsed show. I knew this because I had individually interviewed each member of the team on the phone before the session. Maybe because the telephone provided a level of anonymity, or maybe because they just needed to vent to someone neutral, I got an earful from every one of them.

"He would sell his own mother out if that would get him ahead."

"It's all about Jasmine's world—she's the center of her own universe."
"Our boss thinks this has nothing to do with him, but he is enabling all the bad behavior."

I knew there was more to this team than met the eye. So I waited and watched for signs of trouble.

I soon realized one of the team members was obviously uncomfortable with the whole premise of a session on team effectiveness. Unfortunately, instead of putting his cards on the table, he used sarcastic comments to try to undermine the process and me as the facilitator. His self-protective behavior told me that he had something to protect. I was already starting to see the other side of the team.

The next warning sign was the sickeningly sweet behavior of the team member everyone had identified as the bully. He was doing his most endearing "I'm just in it for the team" routine. He'd obviously succeeded in fooling the boss while quietly undermining his teammates. Again, nothing was said directly; it was all just hanging in the air.

Where there's a bully, there must be a victim. I found her pretty quickly, too. She was more than happy to betray her teammate on the phone with me, but given the opportunity to raise concerns in this open forum, she kept quiet. Even with considerable encouragement from me, she spoke so indirectly that the punch failed to land. She didn't have the courage to tell the bully about the damage he was inflicting.

And all this drama seemed to be lost on the team leader. He seemed naïve and overly optimistic that a good discussion would turn things around. He had no emotional connection to everyone else's distress. I imagined him as a suit-and-tie version of Rodney King, saying, "Can't we all just get along?" Unfortunately, the answer was "no," and he didn't have a plan B.

With this team, trying to get something accomplished was a disaster. Those with power would ram things through while those without would watch in frustration. But unlike a Spectator team where those decisions would have stuck, in this passive-aggressive team people used back channels to overturn or at least stall the implementation of decisions that had already been made.

I was dealing with a Bleeding Back team, and the scars from the knife wounds were still fresh. This passive-aggressive type of team appears polite, but is brutal in its own way. There is no overt conflict, but any consensus created in the room is false consensus. A Bleeding Back team takes conflict underground. Members secretly reopen decisions or simply fail to carry them out. No one knows where they stand, and no interaction can be trusted.

> Bleeding Back Team: A team where conflict and differences of opinion are expressed through passive-aggressive means such as humor, gossip, and back-channel decision making.

CIVILITY

Steve Jobs aside, the vast majority of successful people have learned how to behave in polite company. I had my struggles adapting. I grew up in a family where my dad would regale us with old Air Force songs and where we spent one Christmas reciting the definitions of swear words from our brand new dictionary. Then I spent five years in graduate school where professors taught us the art and sport of trashing a colleague's research. So I was a little behind on the airs-and-graces front. I had to learn my manners from colleagues who taught me which fork to use at charity galas and how to cock my head to the side to appear interested in the incessant rambling of a table companion. I learned how to make nice.

Later in my career, an assessment tool pegged my political savvy at the fourth percentile, just slightly above people who make a pass on the boss's wife at the holiday party. In the years since, I have certainly adjusted my style to improve my connection with others. At the same time, I sometimes choose to challenge a culture that insists on handling every interaction with kid gloves. I fear that an organization that doesn't allow open conflict will still have conflict—it will just happen in the shadows.

A healthy dose of civility is a good thing. Sometimes we need to be gracious and let our colleagues save face. But civility can't just be an excuse for passive-aggressive behavior. And that's what's really going on in too many teams who consider themselves *nice* people. They aren't nice at all; they're just too chicken to stab you in the front.

ORIGINS OF A BLEEDING BACK TEAM

A Bleeding Back team can develop slowly, or it can come about in a quick and deadly spiral downward. Sometimes the origins are completely innocent. A comment gets misinterpreted as hostile, a message gets passed on incorrectly, and suddenly you're walking through a minefield. Here are a few problems that create a Bleeding Back team.

Inability or Unwillingness to Give Feedback

Poor communication skills are the most fundamental problem on a Bleeding Back team. As a child, adults probably chastised you if you tried to give feedback to a friend or teacher: *"Johnny, we don't say things like that."* If you had a grandmother like mine, you probably learned that if you can't say anything nice, you shouldn't say anything at all. Unfortunately, this didn't change your opinions about the things you observed; it just taught you not to express them—at least not until you were safely at home. The adults in your life trained you to be passive-aggressive.

It's no surprise, then, that people in organizations think it's not nice to criticize their teammates—at least not to their faces. Even if you believe that providing constructive criticism is helpful, you probably don't know how to give the feedback in a way that's palatable and feels supportive. You've probably had a few bad experiences where someone got defensive, angry, or emotional. You're probably justified if you feel like it's easier to not give feedback at all. But that inability to say what you mean helps create a Bleeding Back team.

Low Trust and Safety

Lack of trust also makes your team susceptible to a Bleeding Back problem. When you don't trust one another, you and your teammates don't know where you stand and don't feel confident enough to challenge issues openly. Sometimes the trust issues are between individual members of the team. Maybe you've heard your teammate has spoken badly of you to the team leader without raising the issues with you first. Now you probably don't feel much like engaging directly with her. You might resort to criticizing her behind her back.

Sometimes, the trust issue starts with your team leader. When he scolds or mocks a team member for making a negative comment or sharing a criticism, the team becomes a very unsafe place to be candid. If your boss has an implicit or explicit expectation that members of the team need to be a united front, you won't feel safe voicing concerns openly for fear of being branded a naysayer. Regardless of whether you feel leery of your teammates or of your team leader, if trust is in short supply on your team, you better watch your back.

Back Channels

Decision-making loopholes also contribute to the development of a Bleeding Back team. It's a lot like what happens when parents have different ideas about raising their children. If the kids learn that a "no" from Mom can be overturned by batting eyelashes at Dad, they'll go behind Mom's back to get what they want. The same happens with passive-aggressive team members. If fighting for what you want openly doesn't work, but lobbying the boss or other key players outside the room does, you'll learn to stick with that bad behavior.

There are deep-seated and complicated reasons for the passive-aggressive behavior on your team. Unfortunately, most workplaces try to solve this problem with an incredibly unhelpful solution: hanging values plaques on the wall like they're hanging garlic to ward off vampires. These posters and plaques tend to encourage false harmony and a façade of politeness, but they do nothing to deal with the underlying trust or communication issues. Those issues don't emerge in meeting rooms; they emerge in washrooms and behind closed office doors—where somehow the values don't seem to apply.

IMPACT OF BEING A BLEEDING BACK TEAM

Bleeding Back teams are incredibly destructive both to the members of your team and to your organization. Unfortunately, it can take a long time to identify this problem, because superficially the team looks healthy. And by then, your team and organization are already suffering the effects, such as:

Poor decision making. To make good decisions, you need access to all the information that will help you understand the issues. On a Bleeding Back team, your teammates don't openly share the information, concerns, or criticisms they have. As a result, the decision-making process feels deceptively smooth. It's easy for you to develop a false sense of security. With little overt resistance, you make decisions quickly, but they're based on an incomplete picture that excludes critical information. This skewed perspective isn't obvious until the execution fails. By then, it's too late.

Slow implementation. Although decision making on a Bleeding Back team can be much quicker than on other teams, you lose the advantage because it takes forever to implement the plan. Before the decision becomes reality, your team members rehash it through back channels. The plan you thought was signed, sealed, and delivered is still being actively resisted by people you thought were on your side. Even if they don't succeed in reversing the decision, they'll probably manage to delay implementing it, and then they'll do only the absolute minimum required to look like they are complying. If it's really bad, they'll wait for you to fail and then smirk and say, *"I told you so."* If your team doesn't fully discuss and debate an issue before making a decision, you can expect a much bumpier ride when you try to execute.

Inter-team confusion. Bleeding Back teams make terrible collaborators, because people outside the team can't make heads or tails of what is going on. You and your teammates probably hide criticisms and concerns from one another, but share them freely with people outside the team. Now imagine that someone outside your team gets a full rundown on a particular project from you, and then gets an earful of complaints from your teammate; who can they believe? How often have you been in that situation with other teams in your organization? You think you understand the story and then someone else paints a completely different picture. All you can say is, *"You guys need to get in a room together, work this out, and then tell me what you need me to do."* That team loses credibility in your eyes. Now remember that if your team is causing conflict outside the team instead of inside, you're losing credibility, too.

Bleeding Back teams also take a deeply personal toll on their members. I was once on a Bleeding Back team, and I felt like I didn't know who I could trust or where I could turn to make things better. I dusted off my resume and starting taking interviews with recruiters because I couldn't stand the seething resentment hidden just below the surface of the team. Thankfully, I had a few good conversations with my boss, and he rectified the situation before I jumped ship.

Mistrust and second guessing. When you've seen your teammates overturn or ignore a team decision a couple of times, you start to get paranoid about everything everyone says. You see them nodding their heads while you're talking, but you know they did that the last time, too. Then someone tells you that the people who were nodding in the meeting were mocking your ideas behind your back at lunch the other day. Soon you don't feel confident in even the most secure of your relationships. If your team is a team of managers, you'll probably pass this mistrust down to your direct reports—eventually spreading the clan war throughout the organization.

On a Bleeding Back team, it's hard to find someone to talk to in confidence. If you need to think through a situation or get some advice about an adversarial teammate, you have to choose your confidante carefully, so she doesn't turn around and blab what you said to others. The whole scenario tends to drive you away from your team and toward people outside with whom you can talk more candidly.

Stress. This all adds up to a very stressful experience. You spend tons of energy trying to decode the messages coming not only from what people are saying, but also from what they're not saying: their body language and other subtle cues. You have to do an inordinate amount of extra work to move things forward because each person needs to be presold on an idea—so you have to do a round of politicking before the official discussion begins. If your boss is part of the problem, you may be getting negative feedback in the form of cutting humor or sarcasm. Or maybe you're just stuck watching the plum assignments go to other people. Being on a Bleeding Back team is highly stressful and a significant risk to your physical and mental health.

DIAGNOSTIC

Recognizing a Bleeding Back team requires a combination of good watching and listening with a good dose of intuition. If you just listen, you won't usually hear a problem. It's when the actual results and actions of the team don't line up with what is being said that you can start to see through a Bleeding Back problem. Use the diagnostic test in Figure 6.1 to assess the level of risk on your team.

TRIAGE AND EMERGENCY MEDICINE

Navigating out of the minefield of a Bleeding Back team will take a lot of time and a lot of patience. Because trust has been eroded, your teammates will view even constructive actions skeptically. It can be disheartening when teammates are dubious, but hang in there. Even small progress will be welcome relief.

If you are the team leader or the team leader is on board:

1. *Decision-making rules.* You can start to fix things with structural and process changes. Start with the decision-making process. Set out the rules of engagement for decisions, with particular attention to when and where it is acceptable to disagree with the proposed course of action. If the team usually moves too quickly, introduce a timeline that provides ample opportunity for people to raise concerns. For example, don't open and close decisions in a single meeting. Provide time for people to raise legitimate concerns so they aren't tempted to take these concerns behind closed doors.

    You'll also need to set expectations for what happens after a decision is made. If your team is going to be open to reversing decisions within a certain statute of limitations, set

	Symptoms	True
Early Warning	We refrain from making comments that might be uncomfortable to others.	☐
	We use very indirect language when we disagree.	☐
	Team members seldom air their frustrations in team meetings.	☐
	We keep up appearances that we get along.	☐
	My team leader blames difficult decisions on others outside the team.	☐
Moderate Case	We use humor to deflect feedback or criticism.	☐
	Sarcasm and nasty humor is used against teammates.	☐
	Members of the team complain about each other behind closed doors.	☐
	My team leader allows people to reopen decisions after they are made.	☐
	Dissent is not allowed in our meetings.	☐
Severe Case	My team leader allows people to complain privately about team members.	☐
	We are not held accountable if we fail to implement a decision.	☐
	My team leader changes decisions without bringing them back to the team.	☐
	We allow people outside the team to get caught in our battles.	☐
	We regularly make decisions and fail to implement them.	☐
	Total	—

Figure 6.1 Bleeding Back Team Diagnostic Test

out the ways a decision can be overturned (e.g., requires a formal team meeting, requires that two-thirds of the team agree with overturning it). If you are not going to allow decisions to be reopened, make that very clear. Passive-aggressive behavior flourishes when people can avoid the discomfort of disagreeing publicly but still enjoy the benefit of having their opinions heard. If your decision-making process closes that back door, the bad behavior will taper off.

2. *Escalation process.* You'll also need formal procedures for how to handle disagreements among members of the team. Too many people take their beef straight to the team leader without ever speaking directly with their teammate. Your team leader needs to insist that no issues come to her until they have been aired with the teammate first—except in the case of abusive behavior, where it is entirely appropriate to seek help through formal channels. If you and your teammate can't fix the situation on your own, then you can go to your boss for coaching and advice. I still recommend that you deal with the issue yourself, but your boss will now be aware that there is an issue and can support you in dealing with it.

   If, and only if, attempts to resolve the dispute on your own do not work, then your team leader should bring the involved parties into her office together and seek a way forward. This is a last resort because it demonstrates that you don't have the wherewithal to solve your own problems. Ideally, you won't need as much help the next time. An escalation process that requires team members to attempt to address their own issues before involving the boss will significantly curtail harmful backstabbing behavior.

   The finance management team from the beginning of the chapter used a formal escalation process to curtail the number of disputes going directly to the team leader. Individuals on the team had to take responsibility for their relationships with their teammates.

It is sad but true that team leaders often cause, or at least reinforce, Bleeding Back behavior. It might suit your conflict-avoidant boss just fine to keep the aggression below the surface. More likely, your team leader just doesn't want to hear that there is a problem. Then you have to hope that your teammates are ready to start with a clean slate.

If your teammates are on board:

1. *Set the tone.* Often Bleeding Back behavior occurs because people aren't willing to open themselves up to direct feedback. Defensiveness makes it seem more palatable to complain behind closed doors. If your team is ready to make things better, you can actively solicit different points of view. Ask people to help make your ideas better. Highlight perspectives that you don't feel you've covered adequately and see if people can offer any expertise. Even if the boss is lobbing sarcastic one-liners at you, if the team is willing to discuss the issues directly, the dialogue will become more constructive.

2. *Make room for dissent.* How you react to frank comments will determine whether early attempts at direct feedback gain momentum. Your team needs to practice staying open and curious and really try to hear and understand what everyone is saying. Use broad, open-ended questions to understand the other person's perspective: *"Help me understand what makes you uncomfortable about the proposal." "What do you see that I've missed?" "How would you look at this problem differently?"*

   To make it really clear that you are willing to turn over a new leaf, thank your teammates when they say something uncomfortable. *"I hadn't thought of it that way, thank you."* You don't have to pretend you love the criticism, but you can be grateful that it came out in public where you have a chance to do something with it, rather than being whispered behind your back. If you have a private moment to say thank you, try being authentic. *"That was really difficult for me to hear so I'm guessing it was hard for you to say it. I'm grateful you did."*

In my experience, the first two scenarios aren't very common. Unless the team has been through a formal team-effectiveness process, your teammates probably aren't going to spontaneously start confessing to stabbing people in the back. Fortunately, if you calmly and deliberately confront every example of passive-aggressive behavior you come across, you can change a Bleeding Back team on your own.

If you're on your own:

1. *Shut down gossip.* One of the best ways to change the dynamic on your Bleeding Back team is to start taking the high road. When someone gossips to you, shut it down. How you shut it down depends on whether you think the person's point has merit or not. If it doesn't, ask some questions to help your teammate see the issue a little more objectively. Chastising him won't do any good. Just be supportive and help him look at the situation from another perspective: *"I don't think that's what Michael meant by his comment. What do you think he was really trying to say?"*

   If, on the other hand, you believe there is some truth to your teammate's concerns, you need to take a different tack. Your goal here is to get the issue out into the open so it can be resolved. Share your concerns and then help the person find an appropriate forum to deal with them. *"I agree with you that Michael's comments were inappropriate. Would you like me to help you think through how you will address it with him?"* If it's a team issue, suggest including it on the agenda for an upcoming team meeting. Either way, your teammate will see that you are serious about making the team healthier.

2. *Call it in the room.* Last, if you're brave enough, call out passive-aggressive behavior when you see it. When a teammate rolls her eyes, say, *"From your reaction, I get the sense you disagree. What are you thinking?"* Sometimes it's the absence of a reaction that you need to call out. *"I'm really surprised*

that no one is commenting. I expected this to be a contentious issue. What aren't you saying?" When someone uses humor against you, let everyone have their laughs, then say, *"Sounds like there's actually an important point under that joke. What should I be taking from it?"*

The most amazing thing happens when you stand up to passive-aggressive behavior. Suddenly everyone else's child-ishness is laid bare. And the vast majority of people will feel self-conscious about how they've been acting. When they learn that they can't get away with it (with you, anyway), they'll very quickly start acting like grownups. We humans are pretty conformist, so giving your teammates a positive role model to conform to will work wonders.

Being nice and respectful to your teammates is an honorable goal. We could all stand a little more kindness in our lives. But it has to be authentic respect and genuine kindness, not cowardly public civility that hides vicious gossip in private. Hidden conflict is insidious and traps us in endless cycles where bad behavior creates mistrust and mistrust creates bad behavior. If you are part of a Bleeding Back team, you need to get differences of opinion out in the open where you can harness them to move you forward. Otherwise you're doomed to take one step forward and two steps back forever.

CHAPTER 7

The Royal Rumble Team

The minute I walked into the room for the strategy session with a high-tech company, I felt the buzz. It was a magical combination of intellectual and physical energy. The intellectual energy came from the thrill of cracking vexing technical challenges. They had recently made a big breakthrough on a technical design and they were charged by the attention they were getting from analysts. The physical energy came from the high-strung personalities. These men had probably been the boys who drove teachers to distraction with their fidgeting. The Diet Coke for breakfast and candy all day long probably didn't help.

We had a lot to tackle in our two-day strategy session. The team faced an incredibly difficult decision that's all too common in the tech sector: When is it time to stop investing in our cash cow business so we can throw the weight of the organization behind our disruptive new technology? The problem, described beautifully in Clayton Christensen's book, *The Innovator's Dilemma*, is that diverting resources away from the old product will hasten its demise, while revenue from the new product probably won't grow fast enough to bridge the gap. It's incredibly difficult to find the right moment to flip the switch, and the decision requires market data and analytics as well as intuition developed over years in the industry.

The conversation started getting louder and faster. Each person in the room led a division or department and they staunchly defended their teams and products. The sheer brainpower around the table was staggering. Things moved quickly and every argument was matched by a clever counterargument. It reminded me of those Greenwich Village chess matches where each player moves definitively and then slaps the timer to pass the play to their opponent.

Click of the chess piece on the board. *Thwap* on the timer. *Click.*
Thwap. Click. Thwap.

Tension started to build between the team member representing the old product line and the one responsible for the new. I could
see it in how they were playing with the Silly Putty I'd put on the
tables. Recent neuroscience research has found that giving people a
tactile toy to play with can promote attention in long meetings—
that's why I use it. But I have learned that it also gives me clues to the
state of mind in the room because there is a telltale "snap" when
tensions run high and team members start to take out their aggression on the putty.

Shortly after I noticed the rising emotional tenor of the room,
one of the team members stood up and started pacing while talking;
soon another followed suit. Before I got everyone refocused, there
was yelling, table pounding, and plenty of swearing.

The discussion became increasingly polarized. They weren't
talking about the timing of the anticipated drop-off in sales anymore. Instead, it was personal: *"You've been saying it's going to drop
off for years. You've been wrong over and over!"* Some members of the
team jumped in on one side or the other. A couple tried to share
points that might open up the discussion. Others just pushed back
from the table and rolled their eyes—they had heard this debate
before.

For his part, the team leader wasn't fazed. He's a competitive
guy and he saw these heightened emotions as a sign that everyone
understood how urgent the problem was. He remained calm and
rational. His judgment wasn't clouded by the emotions in the room.
If only that were true of his team.

The two quarrelling team members, each of them senior
leaders in the organization, were not making arguments about the
best interest of the company; they were making arguments about the
best interest of their pet projects. Their passion had so fully clouded
their judgment that they couldn't even hear the merits of their

teammate's case. It was no longer about what was right for the company—it was all about winning the pissing match.

This team had definitely become toxic. They had become a Royal Rumble team, fighting purely on emotion and letting all that intellectual firepower go to waste. When a team channels its passion into personal combat, they waste all their energy on fighting the competition inside rather than the competition outside. Sure, it can feel good to be engaged and vigorous, but no matter how high you rev the engine, if your wheels keep spinning, you're not going anywhere.

Royal Rumble Team: A team where passion and enthusiasm are misdirected into personal and unproductive conflict between members of the team.

ENGAGEMENT

In the past several years, the topic of employee engagement has regularly appeared in the headlines. Engagement, we're told, is the secret to unlocking discretionary effort and improving productivity. Studies show that too many employees are checked out; they just show up to collect a paycheck and go home. Economists have even coined the term *presenteeism* to describe people who are physically at work, but mentally and emotionally absent.

I work with so many comatose teams that when I meet a highly engaged team, I'm thrilled to see people who are invested in their work. I'm relieved when people give a darn enough to fight for what they believe. I'd rather be in a room where people are hollering than where they're snoring. I am happy for you to talk all you want. You just can't forget to listen.

If you're engaged, but only with *your* project, *your* ideas, or *your* vision of the future, you are not listening to the information that would help you understand what's right for your *team*, your

organization, and your *customer*. When what's right for you gets disconnected from what's right for your team, you start to disengage and get defensive. Once your back is up, you stop listening and start working at odds with your teammates.

When you let your personal passions get the better of you, when you get too invested in ideas because they're yours, then you lose all the benefit of high engagement. Your team needs to channel its passion to beat the competition, not to beat up on one another.

ORIGINS OF A ROYAL RUMBLE TEAM

People are usually surprised to learn that I spend more time trying to nurture conflicts than I do trying to extinguish them. But productive conflict focuses on issues, not individuals. How do you tell the difference? Unhealthy conflict sounds different. The word "you" gets used a lot—as in "you didn't" or "you should." People talk a lot about the past—about "last time" or what "never" or "always" happens. The conversation gets quicker. The tone becomes more aggressive. Louder, deeper voices start asserting themselves over the rest of the team. Some people display aggressive body language, leaning in and pounding on the table, while others start to look defensive, leaning back, folding their arms, and avoiding eye contact.

Here are several factors that contribute to a Royal Rumble team. Recognize any?

Emotional Intelligence

Interestingly, Royal Rumble teams can emerge when you have either too little or too much emotional intelligence. The case of too little emotional intelligence is probably more common. Some people are smart and powerful, but are willing to use brute force to get their ideas adopted. I see this frequently in C-suite leaders and technical experts who can think circles around their teammates, but don't have the patience to help them understand. Are you ever guilty of trying to baffle or belittle your teammates into agreeing? How often do your teammates roll over? How often do they go the Royal Rumble route and fight fire with fire?

Or is the problem on your team too much emotional intelligence—shrewd and calculated attempts to push one another's buttons? Have you and your teammates learned that the right attack can render the opponent flustered, upset, and inarticulate? Do you use power to cut down someone who might have had a valid concern? Thinking of emotional intelligence as a uniformly positive force is naïve. Like most intelligence, emotional intelligence can be used for good or evil.

Bad Meeting Management

I'm not suggesting that you need to model your team meetings on the British House of Lords, but meetings lacking in some basic decorum go downhill quickly. For example, frequent interruptions mean you respond without hearing what your teammates are saying. Often, this means you're reacting based on incomplete information, which can lead to bad assumptions and misplaced aggression.

Getting away with making issues personal can also create a Royal Rumble problem. If you are attacked by a teammate and no one comes to your defense, you might feel that you need to counterattack to defend yourself. Let the games begin. If the meeting had been well managed, the person who lobbed the personal attack would have been corrected and you would not have felt the need to reciprocate. Even if your teammate was looking for a fight, it's hard to have a one-person rumble! If your team has a weak meeting chair, you are vulnerable to a Royal Rumble problem.

Individual Rewards and Recognition

It never fails. The organization that has plastered its walls with cheesy teamwork posters of rowers, mountain climbers, and jets flying in formation is the same organization that has a bonus and incentive scheme based solely on individual contribution. If you create a culture of heroes and zeros, you motivate team members to fight to win. Individual rewards and recognition remove the incentive to cooperate and increase the incentive to compete.

Working with the team in the opening story of this chapter, I really felt for the guy leading the legacy product line. He supported the tough call to divert resources away from his product line to fund the new projects, and then his teammates used his declining sales as ammunition against him. *Seriously?* The entire profit and loss structure made it more logical to fight against his teammates than to work with them. When organizations naïvely expect individual goodwill to be a more powerful motivator than their rewards systems, they get the Royal Rumble teams they deserve.

IMPACT OF BEING A ROYAL RUMBLE TEAM

Being a part of a Royal Rumble team is great if you're an adrenaline junkie. It can be invigorating to get so fully into your work. But if you get too invested in one side of the debate, you shut out different points of view and reduce the quality of the discussion. Unable to effectively harness the energy in the room, your Royal Rumble team faces several serious challenges, including:

Slow decision making. Royal Rumble teams take a really long time to make decisions. It's surprising they are so slow, because the energy in the room makes it look like things are happening. But all the action is back and forth and none of it is forward. A Royal Rumble dynamic leaves no room for compromise, so the universe of solutions is pretty much just Option A and Option B. If you're for Option A, you'd rather do nothing than endorse Option B, while all of your teammates supporting Option B feel the same about Option A. In the end, *nothing* is exactly what will happen.

Often your team will just postpone the decision, hoping some external force will change things and suddenly make the right decision more obvious. Imagine how easily a Royal Rumble team can develop a Crisis Junkie problem if a crisis is the easiest way to force the hand of one side or the other. Royal Rumble to Crisis Junkie is the modus operandi of the U.S. Congress.

False choices. When you fight over who's right and who's wrong, you force a choice that's probably not the right choice or even a necessary choice. When you get entrenched in opposing points of view, you can't see that some combination of solutions is possible. Particularly in strategic discussions, this false dichotomy can really limit thinking. Many great strategic breakthroughs have come from accomplishing seemingly opposing goals. If the Southwest Airlines team had been a Royal Rumble team, they never would have thought it possible to be the cheapest airline *and* the airline with the highest customer satisfaction ratings. One side would still be fighting for cheapest and the other for friendliest, like the guys in those old Chunky Soup ads who spent years fighting over the right utensil to use: "Fork!" "Spoon!"

Turnover. There is only so much abuse you can take before you decide it's not getting better. At some point, you or your teammates will give up and leave a Royal Rumble team. The aggressors leave because bullying isn't working. Perhaps there are easier opponents somewhere else. The bullied leave because they're tired of being punching bags. Even the witnesses get fed up and leave because they're sick of getting nothing done. With any luck (and a better selection system), the replacements might be a little more open minded. But if the replacements just take up the vacated posts as leaders of Camp A and Camp B, you're going to find yourself right back in the middle of the ring. The Royal Rumble team is bad for your organization and it's bad for you, too.

Embarrassing behavior. If you get sucked into a Royal Rumble dynamic, you had better hope that no one is using their smartphone to record you. If your fight-or-flight switch lands in the fight position, you'll spew lines that would be really embarrassing to relive later. People say things that are silly, hurtful, or downright inane because they think they will sink their opponents. Once you get a reputation for this kind of behavior, it will precede you. Not only that, but you will find it difficult to look yourself in the mirror. Barroom brawling is bad enough. Don't embarrass yourself with boardroom brawling.

DIAGNOSTIC

It doesn't exactly take sensitive instruments to detect a full-fledged Royal Rumble problem on your team. In fact, a decibel meter in the room would probably do the trick. But if your problem is just starting to brew, you might pick it up with some of the warning signs in the diagnostic test in Figure 7.1.

TRIAGE AND EMERGENCY MEDICINE

If your team has started to show signs of a Royal Rumble problem, you might still have time to reverse the trend before the only solution is a public battle to the death in the front lobby. The approach you take depends on who on your team is willing to take off the gloves.

If you are the team leader or your team leader is on board:

1. *Set the rules of engagement.* A good first step toward improving a Royal Rumble team is to develop a set of rules that

Symptoms		True
Early Warning	We talk over one another and interrupt often.	☐
	We make discussions personal rather than focusing on the issue.	☐
	We defend mudslinging as healthy debate.	☐
	We raise our voices at one another.	☐
	We defend our own positions and fight for functional perspectives.	☐
Moderate Case	We disagree in factions, with team members taking sides.	☐
	We point fingers and blame a scapegoat when we fail.	☐
	We react to comments without really hearing what others are saying.	☐
	Our disagreements are very black and white with no middle ground.	☐
	My team leader tolerates negative comments targeted at individuals.	☐
Severe Case	People scream and yell at one another in our meetings.	☐
	We use insults and offensive language directed at one another.	☐
	Some members of the team withdraw completely from arguments.	☐
	My team leader participates in partisan arguments.	☐
	We go around and around on the same issues without resolution.	☐
	Total	____

Figure 7.1   Royal Rumble Team Diagnostic Test

will govern your behavior. The basic idea is to start listening to one another. Stipulate that only one person talks at a time. Make a rule that before starting a new point, each team member has to paraphrase what the previous speaker said. Until the first person agrees that their ideas have been appropriately summarized, the second person is not allowed to move on. I watched two members of a team go back and forth three times before the first person was really heard. Immediately team members realized how poorly they were listening and slowed down.

More advanced tactics focus on how to handle major differences of opinion. You can require that everyone weigh in on where they are—take a straw vote to see how far you are from a decision. You can set time allowances for how long the debate will continue before you make a decision. And you'll need to set decision rules in advance so that at the end of the debate period, you know whether the team leader will be making a decision or whether a vote will be taken.

2. *Hold people accountable.* There is no point in setting rules of engagement if no one is going to follow them. Your team leader needs to be prepared to hold you accountable when you and your teammates break the rules. Minor infractions should be met with a reminder about the team's commitment to not interrupt or to keep the discussion focused on issues rather than individuals, such as, *"I realize that this is a really important and contentious discussion—all the more reason for us to listen to one another carefully."* More significant missteps need to be called out in the meeting and also addressed privately after the session. If the team leader ignores indiscretions and fails to enforce the rules, they'll become moot.

I like to use humor to set and enforce rules of engagement. If your team has a few bad habits, try giving them a name. One team I worked with referred to their tendency to rapidly volley back and forth with increasing intensity and decreasing courtesy as their "Ping-Pong problem." They found a red Ping-Pong paddle that any member of the team could raise to call out this behavior. The use of the silly term and the relatively gentle rebuke of the paddle made it easy and even kind of fun to enforce the rules. What is your team's bad habit, and how can a little levity help you wrestle it to the ground?

Most team leaders understand that their meeting rooms shouldn't be free-for-alls. But if your boss really is less Bruce Banner and more Incredible Hulk, appealing to the Hulk's better judgment isn't going to work. If you can't get your team leader to behave like a grownup, there is a good chance that your teammates are fed up and ready for more mature behavior.

If your teammates are on board:

1. *Break the stalemate.* The biggest problem on a Royal Rumble team is that you're working with limited or even binary options. You have blinders on. It's black or white, yes or no. Encourage your teammates to contribute more options and nuance to the discussion to reduce this us-versus-them atmosphere. Try to understand the benefits of each option and reflect them in a hybrid solution. If each combatant feels like some part of their idea is reflected in a third option, they might feel more comfortable endorsing that solution.

2. *Return to the problem.* A really bad fight takes on a life of its own, straying farther and farther from the original issue. Eventually you can't even remember where you got started. If your team starts getting embroiled in a two-sided argument, try reframing the problem you are trying to solve: *"We're going back and forth on which solution makes sense; let's go back to the problem we're trying to solve. How would you*

describe the issue?" Going back to basics might show you that different members of the team were trying to solve different things. Once you agree on the problem, the solution may be easier to see.

You can also try taking some time to talk about how you will make the decision. What are the criteria that you will use to evaluate different options? Can you rank your stakeholders in terms of priority? Is a solution you can implement quickly more valuable than one that takes longer? How much risk is the team willing to tolerate? Sometimes these conversations reveal that one solution is optimal but another solution is acceptable because it works better given the constraints of the situation. In this case, the teammate who proposed the first solution can take solace in the fact that you valued their idea—it might just have been the Cadillac solution when you only needed a Chevy.

Most teams want to behave more maturely; they just need a little help to put old gripes behind them and start over. *Most* teams. Of course, you might be on one of those teams where ego and machismo rule the day. In that case, you are going to have to model grownup behavior in the midst of the madness. First, swap your Diet Coke for a chamomile tea and then try these techniques to stay calm, cool, and collected.

If you're on your own:

1. *Focus on the issue.* The most important thing you can do to counteract the effects of a Royal Rumble team is get the discussion focused on the issues and away from personal criticisms and insults. Each time a teammate points an accusatory finger at someone or makes a personal attack, reframe the discussion around the issue. When someone makes an angry statement like *"You think everything is about your precious sales force!"* try restating it more appropriately: *"We need to think about other key stakeholders in addition to the*

sales team. Who do we need to factor into the equation?" That way, the person talking feels heard but the target of the criticism doesn't feel attacked. If you do this each time, you'll show your teammates they can resolve their issues without resorting to personal attacks.

2. *Be empathetic.* Any plan for rehabilitating a Royal Rumble team needs to start with genuine empathy for the people around the table. It can be very, very difficult to conjure up empathy for the guy who is continually beating his chest or the woman who is always launching into tirades, but that is exactly what you need to do. Aggressive, unseemly behavior is almost always a protective mechanism against some perceived threat. What is the threat? Can you be curious, kind, and empathetic about what has made your teammates feel so defensive?

   If you sleuth out the real issues, you'll be in a much better position to solve the real problem, rather than continually addressing side issues. Does the proposed action threaten your teammate's power or control? Is he secretly worried about being less capable or less successful in the new world? It is truly amazing what a little empathy and curiosity can do to reduce hostility and improve listening around a table. Once you understand the real issue, you can find a solution that moves the team forward without leaving individual team members behind.

Dissent and disagreement can be good for team performance. After all, too much agreement can lead to groupthink. But Royal Rumble teams can't build anything together because their members are too busy tearing one another down. Conflict is too personal and too focused on old wounds. Sure, some of you might prefer this type of outright aggression to the buried conflict of a passive-aggressive team. Some people prefer to be stabbed in the front than in the back. But if you're stabbing one another, no matter where you're doing it, the only people who will be better off are your competition.

CHAPTER 8

The You in Team

A t this point you're probably watching for signs of the different Toxic Team patterns in every team meeting. Maybe you've found one predominant style on your team; you're Crisis Junkies or Bobble Heads. Or maybe you slide into different types of dysfunction depending on the situation. Many people describe their teams as majoring in one dysfunction with a minor in another.

Regardless of exactly how your team is getting it wrong, the second half of this book will show you a clear path to make it better. In each of the Toxic Team chapters, I helped you triage the situation and prescribed some emergency medicine to help you cope in the short term. The rest of this book provides the long-term cure.

You should be cynical right about now. Your team has probably tried a lot of things, spent a lot of time, and wasted a lot of money in a quest to improve your performance. Unfortunately, there haven't been many good answers for you, have there? The team effectiveness landscape has offered you superficial solutions that don't actually target team dysfunction at a level that can create real change. At best, you've been applying Band-Aids.

TEAM BUILDING

The most common answer to a team in need is a team-building session. In these sessions, you put the entire team on a bus, drive until you see trees, and proceed to (a) increase alignment by beating drums rhythmically, (b) foster connection by dividing into sub-teams to race to build something, or (c) increase trust by jumping off cliffs into each other's arms. Team-building activities are great for new teams looking to create shared experiences. They are also great ways to reward a healthy team with a change of pace and some downtime together. But if you are trying to fix an unhealthy team, team-building activities are more likely to make things worse than better. In Toxic Teams these sorts of activities can be downright reckless.

All sorts of nasty stuff emerge when you do these silly exercises with a Toxic Team. I once went to an offsite with a team that cutthroat competition had divided into warring factions. I watched them do a modified Prisoner's Dilemma exercise designed to encourage collaboration. For the game, they divided the team into small groups. Each group secretly decided whether to take a weak or a strong stance in each round. If everyone took a strong stance, all the groups were penalized. If everyone took a weak stance, each got a modest reward—the best outcome for the whole team. If only one group took a strong stance, the strong group was rewarded handsomely while the other groups went without. After lulling the other groups into a false sense of security and getting them on a roll taking weak stances, the boss and his group pounced with a strong stance and collected all the money. Now the team had all the proof they needed that the talk of collaboration was pure BS. Back to square one.

The primary problem with these trite team-building approaches, and even with more serious team interventions, is that they put the onus on the team facilitator or the team leader to just "fix it." Team members often let the discussion wash right over them. Have you ever found yourself in that situation? Have you walked into a team-building session as if you were driving into a car wash—put it in neutral and let the process guide you along until you emerge all sparkly on the other side? Unfortunately, that's not how it works. Let me share an example to explain what I mean.

I once worked with a team of senior marketing people in a large international organization. As is standard in our process, I met with the team leader before speaking with any members of the team. He was a friendly guy, pretty easy to talk to. In that first meeting, he gave me the impression that there were a few issues but that the team was reasonably successful. But something wasn't adding up for me. It was all just a little too casual. The picture he painted didn't line up with what I'd heard from the HR person who'd brought me in. I had scheduled interviews with each of the team members in advance of the first group session, so I knew a more complete picture would emerge. Did it ever.

"Tell me what you believe has led the team to this point," I said. Here's what I heard:

> "Maria is very manipulative and she hoards knowledge so that she has the power. Then she pretends that she just forgot to mention things. Yeah, right!"

> "Our team leader, Robert, just doesn't seem to notice what is going on. Because he doesn't deal with the bad behavior, people think it's okay to continue."

> "Nadi has a pretty big ego. She thinks that the way she does anything is the way everyone should do it. She's just cruising along in Nadi-land oblivious to the rest of us."

Next, I asked what they thought it would take to get the team back on track. They said:

> "I think Robert has to start calling Maria on her behavior. He needs to make it clear to her that she can't shut the rest of us out. If he doesn't, his credibility is really going to suffer."

> "I think Maria needs to stop using her relationships with people outside our team to her advantage. She makes the rest of us look like we're out of the loop."

> "Nadi just needs to get over herself. She needs to think about something other than her own group every once in a while."

Stop now and reread the comments here. What do you notice?

There's one word missing from all of these statements. No matter how long these people spent talking about what led the team to its current malaise or what it would take to fix their problems, not one of them used the word *I*.

IT'S ABOUT YOU

These team members didn't realize or didn't accept that they had played a role in creating their dysfunction. They wanted to just show up at the offsite session and wait for me to make things better. They assumed that I could wave my magic wand and fix Nadi and Maria. Or maybe their team leader, Robert, would just miraculously fix things because he supposedly had power over everyone on the team. Your team leader does have responsibility, but he can't fix things alone. When you focus on how everyone else needs to change, you almost never see the importance of changing yourself.

> You need to realize that you have played a role in creating the dysfunction on your team.

Do you appreciate the role of your own behavior in your team's dysfunction? Have you stopped to consider that *you* might be the closed-minded person on the team? Maybe *you* are the bully. Or maybe you're the one allowing your ideas to be shut down. Do you allow someone to wield power over you? No? If you're confident that you aren't at the center of any of the conflict on the team, is that an excuse to just sit back? Do you just watch these dynamics go on between others? Where do you fit in the story of your team?

Many years ago, while cruising the parenting section of my local bookstore, I had an epiphany that would forever change my understanding of team dynamics. As I looked through the books on raising healthy children, one title caught my eye: *The Bully, the Bullied, and the Bystander*. This 2003 gem was written by renowned child development expert Barbara Coloroso. The title was all I needed, because Coloroso had so beautifully summed up the idea that bullying is a group dynamic. And so it is with dysfunctional teams.

In the years since, I have supported innumerable teams by helping each team member see the role he or she plays in the unhealthy dynamic. I help them understand that they are wounding, wounded, or watching. If one person steps out of any one of those roles it can completely change the dynamic.

With adults in teams, the roles aren't static. Occasionally there's a single bully or one person who plays the victim, but more often, team members switch in and out of roles depending on the situation. Those who are wounded can become aggressive and go on the attack. Those who have been too close to the fire can check out and become witnesses.

When I frame it that way, can you feel the heat? If you have been complaining about your teammates' sins, you need to know that you aren't going to get off scot-free. Regardless of whether you are knowingly or inadvertently hurting your teammates with your words or actions, allowing yourself to be victimized, or passively watching your teammates engage in unhealthy behaviors, you are as responsible as anyone for your unhealthy team and as critical as anyone to changing it for the better.

Sure, you could sit and wait for someone else to make it better, but you might wait forever. Don't you want to improve your life at work? You have the power to make your team more effective. You can change your team.

YOUR RESPONSIBILITIES

The second half of the book reveals the secrets of changing your team. There are five basic responsibilities that you have to live up to if you want to do your part to cure your team of dysfunction. If you can live up to each of the five, you will change the dynamic on your team. If you feel trapped on a Toxic Team, living up to these responsibilities will help you turn things around. If you're just setting out on a new team, that's even better. Practicing the following responsibilities from the beginning will help you avoid the lost productivity and misery of an unhealthy team altogether.

Start with a Positive Assumption: Stop being a victim of your habits and biases. You need to get control of your thoughts and short-circuit your negative assumptions. If you start with a positive assumption, you will be able to listen, learn, and get value from your teammates.

Add Your Full Value: Enough with doing only what you have to do to get along. It's time to really engage with your team. If you bring the benefit of your expertise, your experiences, and your personality, you will be so much more valuable.

Amplify Other Voices: Drowning out minority voices deprives your team of the diversity it needs to make good decisions. If you make room for people and ideas that are normally sidelined, you'll create a much healthier team.

Know When to Say "No": Resist the urge to say yes to every request from your team. If you are more deliberate about what you need to do and more ruthless in saying no to things that will dilute your focus, you will move faster and accomplish more.

Embrace Productive Conflict: Stop wimping out and start having the kinds of difficult discussions that will move your team forward. If you have conflict face to face instead of behind your teammates' backs, you'll spend less time going around in circles and more time getting ahead.

Just because you control the cure doesn't mean I am blaming you for the disease. From working with exhausted, demoralized, and defeated members of Toxic Teams, I know very well that you never meant to end up here. Maybe things just gradually went downhill, or something got said in the heat of the moment that changed things forever. You're under a lot of pressure, and the stress is showing. Sometimes your stress comes from external pressures associated with excessive workloads, broken processes, and unruly bosses. Other times, the pressures are internal and stem from attempts to meet your all-too-human needs. I get it.

Each of the responsibility chapters starts by exposing the forces that make you behave in unhealthy, unproductive, or unsustainable ways. There are different failure paths and you need to understand which you are personally susceptible to before you can make things better. But remember, all I can do is hold up the mirror. You have to do the rest. If you really let the words sink in, some of them may be tough to hear. I know, because immersing myself in these ideas over the past few years has given me some painful moments of self-awareness. I haven't always liked what I've seen in the mirror. My foibles are as evident as anyone's on these pages.

But if you're willing to go there, you'll find it's liberating to understand why you are acting the way you are. If you're behaving badly, it's probably not because you want to. It's more likely that you started using a coping mechanism to survive during a particularly hectic or vulnerable time. Taking a shortcut helped you survive, but now you're seeing the negative effects. Don't worry, it's not too late.

Once you understand why you are showing up the way you are on your team, you can find a healthier way to contribute. With each of the five responsibilities, you'll see what you need to do and why it's so important to live up to your responsibility as a member of the team. But I won't leave you hanging. You'll also find the practical tools you need to implement these new ways of thinking and acting within your team. In many cases, the chapters provide the actual words to say to your teammates and your boss. Each chapter concludes with a quick Health Check quiz that you can use to see if you're making progress and sticking to your resolutions.

As promised, you *can* change your team without the assistance of an expensive team facilitator, without permission from your boss, and even without the cooperation of your teammates. If you live up to these five responsibilities, you will start to change your team all by yourself.

When you do, you will feel the difference. You'll feel good about yourself for taking the high road instead of feeling guilty for taking the easy way out. You'll feel confident that you're adding value to the team instead of feeling blasé about your lackluster contribution. You'll start to notice your teammates' bad behavior getting less and less frequent, and when it does emerge, it reflects poorly on them, not on you. You'll start to see conflict as a necessary part of striving for greatness—still uncomfortable, but necessary and beneficial. You'll wonder why you didn't start sooner.

A word of caution: *Don't try to fix everything at once.* There is a lot in these chapters. The ideas are simple, but applying them is hard. Read the five chapters through and then choose the one that is most relevant to you—the responsibility that will make the biggest shift in your team if you embrace it fully. Spend a few weeks making a conscious effort to move the needle in that one area. Use the tools in the You First Workbook, available at www.ChangeYourTeam.com. They will help you to assess where you are so you can then start making meaningful changes. Once you've mastered one, move on to the next, until you have made all five responsibilities into habits that you practice regularly.

No one responsibility alone will cure a Toxic Team. You can't pick your favorites and ignore the rest. But living up to all five will address any kind of dysfunction you can imagine. For the next five chapters, it's all about you.

CHAPTER 9

Start with a Positive Assumption

We see things not as they are but as we are.
—Talmud

It's Over before It's Begun

It's 10:45 on Wednesday morning. So far, your day is going really well. You've crossed three important things off your to-do list and you're rewarding yourself with a lattee. You are sitting at your computer working on a few finishing touches to the big presentation you have to give on Monday when your e-mail alert flashes in the corner of your screen.

All you see is the name. But that's all you need to see. It's from *that* person: the one person on your team who just rubs you the wrong way. The person who makes your heart rate spike and your palms sweat. Maybe it's because they have always been critical of your work. Maybe they have been downright mean—or maybe just aloof. For whatever reason, you have never felt valued by this person.

Can you think of someone on your team like that? Try to conjure up how you actually feel when you interact with them.

You take a deep breath and open the message.

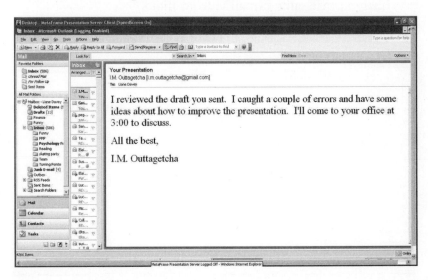

Figure 9.1   Wednesday Morning E-mail Opened—Negative Person

How do you feel?

When I ask this question, most people say things like *"defensive," "worried," "angry,"* or *"annoyed."* But no matter whether they feel anger, sadness, or fear, all agree that they are dreading 3:00.

Now imagine 3:00 comes. How will you behave? Will you sit with your arms crossed looking down at your shoes? Will you sit on the edge of your chair leaning in aggressively over the desk? If you're like most people, you will put up some kind of protective barrier that will create an adversarial dynamic. If you withdraw and protect by distancing yourself, you signal that you don't want to hear what your teammate has to say. If you defend and protect by puffing yourself up, you show that your mind is closed. You're pretty much guaranteed not to hear anything of value your teammate might be trying to share. What a waste.

Now, wipe that person out of your mind. Instead, imagine the teammate who has always been your confidant and supporter. The one you walk out of team meetings with. The one you debrief with at the end of the day. Have you got that person in your head?

Imagine that same e-mail is from them.

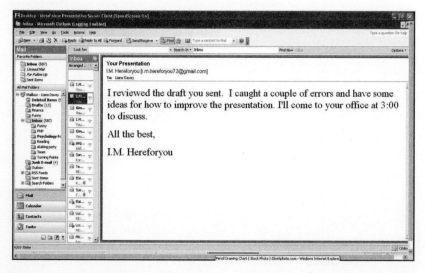

Figure 9.2   Wednesday Morning E-mail Opened—Positive Person

Now how do you feel?

For most people, the response is completely the op-posite: *"relieved," "grateful," "interested," "I'm looking forward to 3:00."*

Really? But it's the same e-mail—why is your reaction so different? *"I'm relieved my friend caught the mistakes before I embar-rassed myself in front of my boss." "I know my colleague is really creative, so I want to hear his ideas." "It's nice that she's offering to come to my office."*

What *is* that? I call it the mother-in-law effect. Can you relate? When I first got married, there were perfectly legitimate things my mother could say to me, but if my mother-in-law said them, I would get pretty defensive.

Person #1 never had a chance, did he? Your guard was up from the moment you saw the name on that e-mail. You unconsciously made a negative assumption about his motives. You could have assumed that he was saving you from embarrassment. You could have believed that he had interesting ideas to share. But your previous experiences and your biases clouded your judgment. You missed your chance to get value from him.

The Brain and Its Dirty Filters

Your brain has about 100 billion neurons, connected by 100 trillion synapses. That's a pretty powerful processor. Fortunately, the vast majority of the work it does happens without your conscious awareness. Your unconscious mind is doing about a million times more work than your conscious mind.

It's efficient, but it's also biased. When a teammate says some-thing, you don't hear it objectively. You filter it through all your past experiences: every nasty comment, every sideways glance, every curt e-mail you've received. Then your unconscious decides how you react.

You react to a comment based on who it's coming from, not what they're saying. The content of the e-mail itself was actually quite neutral, but when it came from someone you don't trust, you focused on the part about finding mistakes and interpreted it as critical. In the case of the person you do trust, you interpreted that same comment as helpful and supportive. All you did was take ambiguous information and use it to either confirm why you don't like your teammate or to reinforce why you do. So, if your starting point is a negative view of one or more members of your team, it's all downhill from there.

Your Conscious Brain to the Rescue

Your conscious mind, and more specifically your frontal lobe, is your great hope for more sophisticated and controlled behavior on your team—and everywhere else, for that matter. In your conscious mind, you can manipulate and work with information. Neuroscientists refer to it as the home of "executive functioning," because it does the work of an executive—it plans, weighs alternatives, and decides.

Your conscious brain has the power to control and override your impulses. It can intercept your fight-or-flight reflex when things get heated on your team and remind you that you are in an office, you are not likely to be eaten, and you should calm down. Once you have control of your immediate impulses, your conscious brain wades through information from all different sources to figure out what is relevant. When you let it in the game, your frontal lobe, the pinstriped executive of your brain, is a really powerful force.

Let's go back to the e-mail example for a moment. Can you see what a difference it will make if you trade in your automatic responses for a more deliberate thought process? Instead of jumping to conclusions about the person's malicious intent, you can suppress your impulse to get defensive, factor in other important information (such as the fact that you asked this person for feedback), and plan to stay open and interested in what they have to say at 3:00. Thanks to your frontal lobe, you can choose to react differently to the e-mail. You just have to let it help.

Reverse the Downward Spiral

When I started to realize that I was falling for the mother-in-law effect, I was pretty disappointed in myself. Why would I assume that my mother-in-law was trying to be anything other than helpful? How could I be so closed-minded? I talk about this stuff every day; why am I not applying it to my own relationships? My filters are as dirty as anyone else's and it takes effort, mindfulness, and practice to work around them.

Negative assumptions and negative reactions can easily create a vicious cycle. Neither you nor your teammate is fully responsible for a disaster, but either of you could have prevented it. Let's go back to that e-mail scenario again. Let's call the person sending out the presentation Rob, and the person sending the e-mail Ingrid.

Rob has an important presentation to give to his boss and the other executives on Monday. He has worked hard on preparing it and feels that he has done a good job. In his weekly one-on-one meeting with Rob, the boss recommends that he send the draft out to his teammates for review. Rob doesn't really want to hear anyone's feedback because he doesn't want more work, but the boss told him to, so he does. Although several team members don't bother to open the e-mail, Ingrid does, and she catches a couple of errors. She also thinks of a couple ideas for Rob, based on other well-received presentations she has seen. That's the point at which our e-mail was sent.

Now the 3:00 meeting happens. Rob is feeling angry and defensive, not to mention annoyed that he has more work to do before Monday. When Ingrid enters his office, she immediately notices that Rob has stayed behind his desk, rather than moving out to the small table where they usually sit. Whether she is aware of it or not, this puts her on guard. She awkwardly pulls a chair from the table and sits across the desk from Rob.

"Thanks for sending me the presentation. Overall, it was good," she says. "I did find a couple of things that I think need to be changed before you share it with the executives."

Rob's inner voice is already starting to be sarcastic. *I bet you did*, he thinks. "Great," he says out loud through gritted teeth.

When Ingrid points out the first calculation error in the table on page 6, Rob makes a note and begrudgingly flips the page. On the next page, she shows him a few typos. On page 13, Rob claims that Acme is their biggest customer, but Ingrid shares recent data that show Omega has taken over the number one spot.

"You caught me again! Is there anything you *did* like about the draft?" he quips defensively. "Maybe *you* should give the presentation on Monday."

"I thought you wanted my help," says Ingrid, confused and a little miffed.

You can imagine where this scene goes from here. By the time Ingrid gets through the mistakes and starts to share her ideas for making the presentation stronger, Rob has completely tuned out. He's feeling defensive, or angry, or embarrassed, or dumb. Whatever he's feeling, he's definitely not keen to hear a few more suggestions. It's probably not much better for Ingrid, who now feels like she wasted her time trying to help him.

"Don't worry about it," she says, "I've got other stuff I need to get to anyway."

The script for this scene was written the moment Rob read Ingrid's e-mail with a negative assumption about her intent—when his brain decided she was a foe and he went into self-protective mode. The negative body language and tone he used when she first entered his office then triggered a less-than-ideal reaction from Ingrid. And off they went into the same downward spiral that begins each time you start with a negative assumption.

It's even more frightening to think that this whole scenario could play out as a silent film without any words at all. Your most basic intentions are converted into body language milliseconds before they become words. Ingrid sees Rob's crossed arms and responds with a furrowed brow. Rob's brain picks up her furrowed brow and dilates his pupils. Words can make this downward spiral worse, but negative words aren't even necessary. If you're thinking something negative, your body language will betray you even if your words don't.

START WITH A POSITIVE ASSUMPTION

There's only one thing that can save Rob and Ingrid now. And there's only one thing that can save you from their fate. The only way to make things better is to *start with a positive assumption*—to clean up your intentions and emotions. It's not easy. Eventually, you will rewire your brain so that your first reactions to your teammates are positive. But before you get there, you will need to train your conscious brain to intercept negative impulses and deliberately, forcefully, wrestle them to the ground and replace them with more objective information and more measured reactions. I'm imagining your frontal lobe in a sweatband and workout wear.

Are you ready to start?

Stifle the Impulse

Before you can focus on a positive assumption, you need to be aware of your negative assumptions. To do this, you have to be in touch with yourself enough to be aware of your emotions, your body language, your heart rate, and anything else that tips you off to an emotional reaction. At the first sign of a red flag, you need to have your own trick to short-circuit the reaction.

Imagine your colleague slips up or makes a mistake. Maybe you have an impulse to laugh, make a snide remark, or get off a one-liner that makes you look smart, powerful, or dominant.

You could do that. Or you could control that impulse. *Zip it*.

If you tend to be a physical person, use your physicality to help you. The moment you feel your body signaling an emotional reaction, force yourself to stop. If you catch yourself leaning forward into an assertive position, sit back. If you feel your fists clench, relax your hands and lay them flat on the arms of your chair. If you fiddle with your pen to discharge anxiety, put it down.

If you do yoga or practice meditation, try using your breathing to control your reactions. You are tuned in to your body and you'll notice if your heart rate suddenly increases. In this case, a deep cleansing breath provides the moment's respite you need to stop the reflex and engage the reflection.

Alternatively, if you're more of a thinker, you can use your inside voice. Create a mantra that buys you time. "Breathe," or "wait," or "calm." I use this technique myself. My word is "listen." The minute that I feel my back getting up or notice that my mind is racing to the perfect rebuttal, I slowly and calmly remind myself to listen.

Let's make that real with an example. You are the operations manager of the Northwest Region in a large national grocery chain. In that role, you sit on the regional management team with the marketing, finance, HR, and merchandising managers. One day, the marketing manager stops by to see you in your office. She puts a piece of paper on your desk. On it is a picture of a paper grocery bag showing your store's logo. "We're switching our stores from plastic to paper," she declares. *Paper*, you think. You immediately imagine a rain-drenched suburban Seattle housewife looking down in exasperation at her soggy bread and bruised apples in a puddle at her feet—the waterlogged paper bag has given way. When you snap back to the moment, you realize that your mouth is open because you're ready to tell her that her idea is stupid.

Then you catch yourself. *Wait*, you think. You close your mouth, take a deep breath, and say nothing. Progress!

Your reactions and stress behaviors are very personal, so the ways you short-circuit them need to be just as personal. How will you catch the almost instantaneous tendency to jump to a negative conclusion? What technique will you use to buy your frontal lobe time to come on line? There is no right or wrong way to go about it. Just find your way. Amazingly, your unconscious brain can be reprogrammed. Soon enough, you'll find that this healthy behavior has become a habit.

WHEN IT'S NOT ENOUGH

Some reactions are too toxic to fix with a couple of deep breaths or a calming mantra. Some reactions create full-on fight-or-flight reactions—what Daniel Goleman calls the "amygdala hijack."[1] This phenomenon is addressed very well in other sources, so I won't spend much time on it here. For our purposes, suffice it to say that if your amygdala gets involved and triggers a release of neurotransmitters and hormones, a couple of deep breaths won't do the trick. On average, it will take about 20 minutes for the hormones to

(continued)

(*continued*)

dissipate and for your conscious brain to get back in control. If you have a reaction this strong, ask for a recess and get some air before re-engaging. Make sure you have some good open-ended questions ready and you're prepared to listen to the answers. When you're ready, go back and be honest: *"I guess I feel really passionately about this topic. I needed a minute to collect my thoughts. Can we start again?"*

Consider the Context

Once you've short-circuited your negative assumption, you can start searching for other relevant information that will help you build your positive assumption. This could be more information about the person with whom you're interacting. It could also be more facts about the situation. Seek out more data to fill in the picture.

Consider the person. What do you know about the person that might help you understand her comments? Is she new to the team and missing some background? Is she in a different role than you and saying something from a different stakeholder perspective? Does she have a different style than you, which causes her to focus on an aspect of the issue you haven't considered?

Back to our paper versus plastic example. Thankfully, you were able to catch yourself before blurting out what a bad idea paper bags are or how dumb your colleague is for suggesting it. Now you can actually think about it. What do you know about her? Oh, that's right, she wasn't with the company in 2003 when you switched to paper and then had to switch back after customer outcry. And, now that you think about it, you remember learning about her profile in the team session and she's a visionary type, an idealist. Hmmm . . . maybe you're starting to understand where she's coming from.

Consider the context. You need to factor in more than just what you know about the person. You also need to think about the context of their comments. What might be happening that affects their perspective or emotional state? It's possible that you don't understand all the pressures they're facing. If something doesn't make sense to you, think about what could be true that would help it make sense.

In the paper versus plastic example, the decision to move from plastic to paper might have very little to do with your teammate. It's possible it wasn't her idea at all. What do you know about the pressures coming from the company's new environmental initiative? Do you remember what the CEO said in his speech last week about it? Was there something about the positive impact on your brand of having paper bags?

The point is that once you actually stop to think, you'll probably see lots of reasons why your teammate might be planning the switch from plastic to paper. If you push yourself to get curious about those reasons, your body language will magically (well, neurochemically) display openness and start a positive exchange between you and your teammate. Curiosity killed the cat, but it saved the team.

Get More Information

Next, use some open-ended questions to evaluate the different possibilities you came up with and reinforce the positive assumption you're building. Look for more evidence to support the idea that your teammate is doing her best. Questions will help you understand where she's coming from. They will also help your teammate see what you are paying attention to. Maybe you'll bring up something she hasn't thought about, and she'll realize she missed something important.

There are so many different areas you can explore with good questions. You can learn more about your teammates and their perspective. You can clarify their intent. You can also get more information about the context and what motivates their actions. But first, you have to stop and think about the assumptions you're making. Once you are aware of them, you can test them out. Some might hold, but others will crumble.

In the paper bag story, you have lots of avenues to explore to better understand your teammate's position. You might want to start with questions about her point of view. *"What makes paper bags attractive to you?"* *"What is your experience with paper bags?"* *"Have you seen the switch from plastic to paper work elsewhere—what made it successful?"* You can also ask about the context and the factors affecting her decision to propose paper bags. *"How does this fit with the environmental initiative?"* *"Who are the main supporters of this initiative?"* You will probably be enlightened by her answers.

WHY NOT WHY?

You'll notice that you don't see one word in my sample questions: *why*. It turns out that the word *why* triggers the part of our brain that wants to explain and rationalize. When we ask someone to tell us why they did something, they immediately look to justify their actions with a sensible story. Rather than sparking the open dialogue we're looking for, *why* locks us into our position. It also triggers very basic patterns from childhood. We hear the word *why* and it's like we've just been caught red-handed with crayon on the dining room wall and someone's yelling, *"Why did you do that!?!"*

If you want to understand why your teammate did something, you just need to get there a little differently. If you use "what" or "how" questions, you're more likely to get insight and less likely to get resistance. *"What led you to that conclusion?"* *"Who did you take into consideration in that process?"* *"How did you arrive at that answer?"* If you're worried about peppering your teammate with questions, you can use the safest version of all, *"Tell me about your decision to abandon that project."* If you really want to know why someone did something, don't ask why. Use other questions that make them reflect, not rationalize.

Listen for Clues

There's no point in stopping your impulses and getting into curious mode if you're not going to use the information you get back wisely. Your very last step to Start with a Positive Assumption is to mine for gold in the answers to your questions. Here are three ways to do so:

Collect the facts. Pay attention to the data your colleague uses to support their case. Did they have information you didn't know about? Did they take something into consideration that you had discounted? Are they defining an important term differently than you would define it? These facts are more fodder. Just be careful. Much of what your teammate is presenting as fact might actually be an assumption, a bias, or an interpretation. And that's where you go next.

Understand the emotions. Try to understand your teammate's feelings. These will come out in the words they choose, the tone and volume of their voice, and the nonverbal cues that they display. How are they experiencing the issue? Is it exciting, anxiety-provoking, or frustrating? Accessing these emotions will help you understand why they're doing what they're doing. You might have assumed they had it in for you, when really they were just uncomfortable or in distress themselves.

Uncover beliefs. The hardest level to listen for is the one that's not even evident to the person who's talking: the beliefs and values that drive their behavior. Listen to what your colleague says and try to figure out what's important to them. How do they see the world? What do they value? What has been disrupted for them that's causing a negative reaction? Again, listening and understanding at this level will make you more generous in your assumptions.

When you first start to be aware of the negative assumptions you're making on your team, it will be a little alarming. Don't worry—we all do it. The important thing to remember is that you can get out of your automatic patterns. You can engage your thinking brain and give yourself the opportunity to make more generous assumptions. When you Start with a Positive Assumption, you will trigger positive, forward movement in your conversations with your team. You watch—your generosity will be returned!

Competence, Reliability, and Integrity of Your Teammates

At the most fundamental level, Starting with a Positive Assumption is about trust. That's the way our unconscious brain analyzes the world and the people around us: friend or foe—trust or don't trust. When you trust your teammates, that first unconscious assumption is a positive one (friend). When you don't trust them, that assumption is negative (foe).

But trust is a very complex concept. Team members often tell me that the members of their team don't "trust" one another, but if I hear that from five people, more than likely they're talking about five different issues. Trust can refer to a very basic level of connection with another person—it's hard to trust someone who you hardly know. It can also refer to the person's credibility and competence. Can they do their job effectively? Are they smart and knowledgeable? At the next level, is the person reliable and can they be counted on? At the highest level, does the person have integrity? Are they honest and do they have good motives? Will they take advantage of me if I'm vulnerable or will they have my back?

Starting with a Positive Assumption requires that you give your teammate the benefit of the doubt at all of these levels.

Connection. Even if you don't know your teammate very well, it's best to assume that he is a decent human being who got up in the morning and came to work to do a good job and make a contribution. This is a safe assumption for the vast majority of the people you will ever come across. Assume he wants to be helpful, tries to be useful, and needs to feel connected—almost all of us human creatures do. The alternative is to treat him with suspicion, to wonder "what's he trying to pull." You know that the minute you start thinking that way, there's nowhere to go but down.

Competence. This is the level where the positive assumption really gets tested. I watch people question the technical skills and credibility of their teammates all the time. Here's my take: It's pretty darn arrogant to sit across the table from someone thinking that they aren't up to the job they have been given. Your boss hasn't chosen to remove the person. So just assume they know what they're doing, even if you don't agree with how they're doing it.

Reliability. Here's where the stakes start to get higher. Can you assume that your teammate is going to come through for you? Can you take it for granted that she won't leave you hanging? Yup, I'm telling you that should be your starting point. Remember, we've already assumed that people get up in the morning and come to work to do a good job. So make sure your default is to assume that your teammates will deliver.

Integrity. Now we're really talking. *Integrity* is a heavy word. Are your teammates honest? Do they say what they mean? Do they stand up for you and the team when no one is watching? Or are they likely to throw you under the bus? This one is hard because the pressures in today's workplace make it easy for our teammates to blame someone else rather than taking the heat themselves. But if you sit across the table from someone assuming that they are going to screw you, you are actually giving them a reason to do it. Isn't it better to give them a chance to surprise you?

Depending on the kind of people you work with, you might find that positive assumptions about competence are easy, but staying positive about integrity is really tough to do in light of bad experiences in the past. Alternatively, you might work on a team where there is no question whatsoever about the people's integrity, but their reliability or competence is questionable. The good news is that you're becoming aware of your biases. You are thinking more rationally and objectively about how you respond to your teammates.

If your team has been on a downward spiral, you might have lots of evidence that your teammates aren't trustworthy. And then it's your choice what you want to do with that information. You can continue on the downward spiral, or you can change the trajectory of your team. You can start again with a positive assumption. Push the reset button. Shake the Etch A Sketch. The next e-mail you get, the next ambiguous statement you hear, the next conflicting opinion you encounter, you can choose to change how you respond. You can inhibit your old reactions, think more fully about the situation, ask good questions, and listen and understand.

If you change your assumptions, you'll change your team.

Maybe you're thinking, *This sounds nice and all, but you haven't seen the team of incompetent underminers I have to work with.* Well, notice that this chapter is called "Start with a Positive Assumption," not "Continue Blindly with a Positive Assumption in Light of Evidence to the Contrary." And I didn't just choose the first title because it's catchier. Starting with a Positive Assumption allows us to hear our teammates and to get value from what they are saying. If, after a full hearing, you can reasonably come to the conclusion that they are incompetent, unreliable, or disingenuous, you need to switch modes.

HEALTH CHECK: ARE YOU STARTING WITH A POSITIVE ASSUMPTION?

Once you have been practicing Starting with a Positive Assumption for a little while, take the test in Figure 9.3 to evaluate how you're doing.

Responsibilities		Yes
Stifle the Impulse	I am more aware of how I react to my teammates.	☐
	I catch myself when I get angry or upset.	☐
	I know what types of things cause me to react and can better prepare.	☐
	I stay in touch with how my body (racing pulse, clenched fists) is reacting.	☐
	I pay attention to my body language and the signals I'm sending.	☐
Consider the Context	When I get upset, I think about the person's intent, not just my reaction.	☐
	When issues upset me, I try to think more broadly.	☐
	I stop to think about the other person and their perspective.	☐
	I take the context into consideration.	☐
	I stay open to possible explanations rather than jumping to conclusions.	☐
Get More Information	I stay open and curious about issues that at first are upsetting.	☐
	I ask questions to test my early thoughts about a situation.	☐
	I use open-ended questions to encourage dialogue.	☐
	I avoid accusatory statements and questions that start with "why."	☐
	I keep my tone positive and show genuine interest in the answers.	☐
Listen for Clues	I listen for facts and information that might be new to me.	☐
	I separate out judgments that are stated as facts.	☐
	I listen for language that helps me understand the person's emotions.	☐
	I pick up clues from the person's body language that show emotions.	☐
	I listen and learn about the person's values to understand them better.	☐

Figure 9.3   Start with a Positive Assumption Health Check Test

YOUR RESPONSIBILITY IN REVIEW

1. You are set up to make assumptions.

   - Your brain makes snap judgments about people and their intent. These judgments are biased by past experiences and baggage.

   - Your conscious mind gives you the ability to control and override your impulses.

   - You need to reverse the downward spiral of negative assumptions.

2. You must start with a positive assumption.

   - Clean up your intentions and emotions. Train yourself to intercept negative impulses and deliberately replace them with more objective information and more measured reactions.

   - *Stifle the impulse.* Become aware of your negative assumptions and stop them before they cause you to react.

   - *Consider the context.* Don't jump to conclusions. Find more information about the person and also about the context.

   - *Get more information.* Use open-ended questions to evaluate the different possibilities. Try to understand your teammate's intent and what motivated their actions.

   - *Listen for clues.* Listen carefully to collect the facts, understand the emotions, and identify the values that lie beneath the surface.

3. Competence, reliability, and integrity of your teammates.

   - Apply these techniques to develop positive assumptions about your teammates at multiple levels.

   - Assume that they want to *connect*, that they are *competent*, *reliable*, and have *integrity*.

CHAPTER 10

Add Your Full Value

S ix insurance executives sat around the table at a strategy offsite. Five of them had spent their entire careers in insurance. They knew the business intuitively and they were extremely influential in the industry. The sixth member of the team, the head of human resources, had joined the organization two months before, after a diverse career that had most recently included a stint as an executive in retail.

This was a team of smart, driven people, always looking for new ways to get an advantage over the competition. They found innovative ways to mine their data for information that would help them answer the central question in insurance: How do you set a rate that's low enough to win the customer's business but high enough to cover the cost of the customer's claims? If you get that balance wrong, you either don't grow because you're too expensive, or you grow unprofitably because you're paying out too much. This team led the industry in developing sophisticated actuarial techniques aimed at getting this balance just right.

The team generated lots of ideas at their planning session. Everyone chimed in with insights, issues, and opportunities. The new head of human resources participated right from the start, but I could see that she was more focused on soaking up information and understanding the business than on trying to impress anyone. After a while, I could see that something was bugging her. I think it took her a little while to put her finger on it—and then she figured it out.

"I haven't heard a single person mention the customer yet," she said. "I don't get it." She was right. The team used the word *customer*, but they used it to describe the insurance brokers who sell the products directly to the policyholders. For someone coming from retail, this was totally bizarre.

"So we think of our distributors as our customers?" she asked.

"That's right. Technically, the brokers own the customer relationship, so we focus on them."

The head of HR clearly wasn't comfortable with the idea that the company depended on its distributors to understand its customers. "What do we know about our policyholders?" she asked. "How many have multiple products with us? Do people usually insure their home and their car with us, or do we get one without the other?"

The rest of the people around the table had priceless expressions on their faces. Their eyes were squinted, their heads tilted, as if to say, *Wow, hmm, good question!* The COO explained that their system assigned a different number to each insurance policy. A customer with both a home and an auto policy had two separate numbers, which were difficult to link together.

From that moment on, the value the head of HR was really going to add on that executive team was perfectly clear. Although she was one of the best HR people I've ever had the privilege to work with, her unique value on that team was her passion for the customer. Over the years that she spent with the organization, she made sure they prioritized changes that would help them understand their customers and improve their products. When I think of a business leader who adds value across the whole enterprise, hers is still the face I picture eight years later.

PALE IMITATIONS

How do you show up at work? Do you bring 100 percent of yourself, or are you on cruise control? Do you catch yourself thinking, "Why bother?" Have you ever been about to comment when a little voice inside your head said, "Don't bother wasting your time," or "That's not my area. What right do I have to say that?"

More and more these days, when I walk into a meeting room, the people sitting around the table seem like pale imitations of the talented, vibrant people I know are in there somewhere. People are just not contributing fully at work. Some of them are holding back, others have nothing left to give. They are giving only what they need to give to get by. They're lackluster for many reasons: cynicism, lack of trust, the sheer volume of work.

Exhaustion

Thanks to our overprogrammed society, you might just be exhausted. Think about the number of hours the average corporate employee spends in meetings. Imagine Ruth, a payroll coordinator. At HR team meetings, Ruth hears lots of important information, but those two hours don't get her any further on running the payroll. And she can't even start when she gets back to her desk, because she's first got to tackle at least the most urgent of the 40 e-mails she received while she was at the meeting. Add to that her company's increasing expectations of faster and faster service, the pressures from finance to reduce errors, and the good old-fashioned stress of a boss who's a jerk, and it's no wonder we aren't seeing the most enthusiastic, sparkling version of Ruth in team meetings.

All of that assumes work is the only thing happening in Ruth's life, but in reality, she probably started the day already tired. If Ruth was up during the night with a sick child, spent 10 minutes wrestling the octopus trying to get a snowsuit on a toddler, dropped said octopus off at daycare, and then spent 45 minutes stuck in traffic on the way to work, even a Starbucks Venti Bold isn't going to put her in a position to contribute fully at the 8:30 team meeting.

Think about how you feel after a really great vacation, or even just a good night's sleep. Think of your high-water level of contribution on your team—the time when you're at your most rested and fully engaged. How often do you even get close to that bar? If the answer is "not often enough," then you aren't living up to your responsibility to your team.

Focus

Don't recognize that description? Maybe you aren't a faded gray version of yourself. Maybe you're at full strength, but you're coping with the volume and complexity of your work with extreme focus. You are a laser beam of intensity aimed at a very specific point. Bombs could be exploding around you, but you've got your sights set on your target and nothing can distract you. People like this are the corporate marines who see work as a battlefield to be survived. They have a narrowly defined version of their role and they stay focused on accomplishing that goal no matter what is happening around them.

Of course, you need to focus to cut out distractions and get stuff done. The research on multitasking makes this point emphatically— lack of focus slows you down. Even when you feel like it's faster to do three things at once, it's not!

On the other hand, being too focused can make you miss important information. On teams, when you're too focused you may overemphasize your individual role and underplay the contribution you make by improving your teammates' ideas. Remember how that thinking leads to a Spectator team.

When you really listen to the discussions among your teammates, what ideas spring to mind that others haven't thought about? How does your particular angle on an issue expose opportunities and threats your colleagues haven't seen? If you treat your team meeting like a surgical strike where you get in, drop your payload, and get out, you're too focused, and you've completely missed the point of having a team.

Cynicism

Okay, so you're overwhelmed. Sometimes you cope by petering out and other times you cope by being overly focused, but that's not the end of the story. You've probably had days where you felt overwhelmed and your first instinct was to just stick to your script and get the hell out. I bet that on some of those days the little voice in your head told you to suck it up and contribute. So you sat up a little straighter, mustered the energy to listen intently, and found a way to add a new point to the discussion. You were just starting to feel good about yourself when someone slammed your point, or worse, slammed *you* for butting in on a topic that's not your area of expertise. *"Great, that was so worth it. Next time I'll keep my mouth shut,"* you thought.

It's hard not to be cynical sometimes. You are doing your damnedest to survive the onslaught of work and keep contributing. And your reward is somebody on your team cutting you off at the knees. It's exasperating, and it's not surprising if you shut down and preserve your energy for the places where you're appreciated. That's the moment when cynicism makes you back away from your responsibility as a member of a team.

Expert Obsession

We are ridiculously obsessed with experts in our society. We're quick to abdicate our own responsibility for solving problems and place all our faith in the word of the supposed expert. But if that expert is sitting across the table from you in a team meeting, relying on her word is just another way to shirk your responsibilities as a member of the team.

If someone else has all the answers, you can tune out. If someone else can be trusted to solve the problem, you can stay focused on your piece of the puzzle. Guess what? That's a trap. Experts can be useful, but within your team, on your day-to-day work, you've got to be careful not to fall into that trap.

Experts are great at solving problems they've encountered before, but fewer and fewer problems in today's world are that simple. More and more problems need to be addressed from different perspectives. You'll need multiple experts to fully comprehend an issue, let alone to solve it. The minute you find yourself thinking that you're not the expert, give yourself a shake. What *are* you the expert on? How can your unique expertise shed light on the issue? If you can't answer that question, what are you doing on the team?

ADD YOUR FULL VALUE

Regardless of all the reasons to give up, shut down, and go into hibernation to preserve your energy, the only way you can live up to your responsibility as a member of a team is to Add Your Full Value. When you use this as your standard, you'll find so many new ways to contribute to your team. You will listen differently; you will see opportunities and threats differently. Perhaps most important, your teammates will see you differently. They will see you as more valuable to the team.

Technical Value

Let's start with the obvious: You need to do the stuff you were hired to do. If you work in an organization of more than 10 people, you probably have some sort of job description. Maybe it's just a few lines your boss scribbled on the back of a napkin at your recruiting lunch, but it probably does the trick. How does your organization think of you? Are you there to help your retail store build an online presence? Are you an expert working on security in your bank? Are you a supply chain coordinator renegotiating trucking contracts? Start with the most basic single sentence that captures the purpose of

your role. Now ask yourself whether you are adding your full value in that capacity.

Be proactive. I'm going to assume that if someone says, *"What are your thoughts about security in our bank branches?"* and you're the security expert, you're going to weigh in with useful information. I seldom see people who aren't doing at least this much, and when that does happen, it's usually more because the team leader isn't willing to deal with performance and competence issues than because the person isn't properly motivated. So, we're assuming that you can add value in your sphere of expertise when called on. But are you contributing proactively?

To add your full technical value, you've got to watch for emerging opportunities and threats through the lens of your technical expertise. Let's go back to our bank security expert for a moment. Call him William. When William gets his chance to present at the team meeting, he shares what he's been working on: *"We've done a great job over the past couple of years improving the security of our branches when it comes to people coming in off the street. We've decreased the number of suspicious persons entering the branches and we haven't had a robbery in six months."* Everyone nods their heads and agrees that the team has done a great job tightening up security.

"Now we have to turn our attention to the back of the branch. The average branch has five nonbank personnel in the back office each day, and we don't do enough to control access or to know who these people are. That's our next priority, and I'd like to share my initial thoughts on how we will tackle this project." This isn't always easy. Even people on the team who supported the first security project might wish that they could now forget about security for a while. But the organization is counting on William to increase security in the branches, and figuring out the next step is part of how he adds his full value.

Cover your angle. You're not always the one presenting a new idea. Sometimes you're listening to your teammates and thinking about how their ideas might be affected by opportunities and constraints you see. You add significant value by covering angles that others might miss.

Back to our bank. William is sitting in a team meeting watching everyone get excited about putting more branches in shopping malls. They're talking about layouts and color schemes and getting carried away selecting cool new touchscreen panels for the tellers. William can either tune out because the discussion doesn't involve him or figure out how it does. He starts running through security scenarios in his head. Being in the mall means staying open longer. How will that affect security? The branch will have two exits, one to the parking lot and one into the mall—that will mean less control.

William decides to engage: *"As I'm listening to the different proposals for the branch layout, I'm thinking about traffic patterns and watching for which ones leave the staff exposed on more than one side. Can we run through the designs with that in mind?"* Suddenly, the team is thinking about the pros and cons of the proposed layouts in a new way.

Stay current. My high school physics teacher had probably been teaching introductory physics for 25 years when I took his 11th-grade class. He was a good teacher, quietly enthralled by the immutable laws of physics and still motivated by his students' gasps each time an experiment worked. What made me laugh was the file folder of yellow lined paper that held his detailed notes for every class. The paper was so faded it was barely yellow anymore, and it was so brittle that he handled each page like the Smithsonian's archivist handling George Washington's letters. He had figured out how to teach 11th-grade physics two decades before, and that's how he would teach it until he retired. I guess he figured that gravity and electricity hadn't changed much.

Unless you're teaching high school physics (and hopefully even if you are!), you need to stay current in your area of expertise. It's easier to rest on your laurels than it is to stay current, because it's so easy to become exhausted, overly focused, or cynical. How often do you read about advances in your area? Do you attend trade conferences or participate in industry associations? Do you understand your field as it is today, or have you let your expertise go stale?

In our Internet-connected world, someone is advancing the thinking in any area you can dream up. Find them, connect, and engage in a discussion about emerging issues in your field. You have a responsibility to push your thinking so that you can bring more value to your team.

Leveraging Experience

Too many people think their value ends with their technical expertise. They think thoughtfully and proactively carrying out their job description is good enough. It's not. If you pat yourself on the back for a job well done as soon as your agenda item is complete, you're selling yourself short. All of your experiences shape how you see the world. Think about these experiences and the unique value they bring to your team.

Companies and industries. If you've worked in a different industry or even a different company, you can create great cross-pollination on a team. Like the insurance company executive with a retail background I talked about at the beginning of the chapter, the insights you bring from one industry to another are very valuable. Some of these ideas may seem obvious to you, but are foreign to your new team—those insights are gold.

I got to take advantage of this when I joined my current organization after leaving a big global consulting firm. Coming from a large firm, I took its staffing model for granted. It seemed only natural to have lots of young junior people do most of the analysis work so a few senior people could focus on the most important ideas and client conversations. But my new company had never used this model, because it had started out as a boutique firm with a small group of very senior professionals. Helping to figure out how the larger-firm model could work here made me look like a star, when all I was doing was transplanting ideas I had already seen in action.

In my example, I moved from one company to another pretty similar one. It's even easier to add value when you move between two different parts of the same industry, such as from a distributor to a manufacturer or from a customer organization to a supplier. In these cases, you can bring huge value by helping your team see things from another perspective.

Imagine that you've just left a large computer company to join the industry-leading manufacturer of hard drives. It's not long before the contempt for the customer becomes clear: *"Can you believe the computer companies expect us to do all the design on how our hard drive integrates with the rest of the components? They pay us like a throwaway vendor and then expect us to be their friggin' R&D department. It's total crap!"*

You realize you have the chance to improve their understanding: *"I think these companies have been so hollowed out that they can't do their own R&D anymore. They're cutting staff like crazy. You might think they're bullying us, but actually, they're dependent on us. Maybe we should have a conversation with them about what this work is worth. I think they have the money—they just don't have the people."* This window into how the computer company is thinking gives your new team a new avenue to pursue.

Other experiences. You don't have to have worked in another industry or even another company to add value from your experience. Experience working in a different function within your company will have taught you valuable lessons. If you've worked on major projects that have exposed you to different types of issues or a different level of risk, that will be a huge help to your team. Any experience that helps you understand what to pay attention to and how to make progress within the culture of your organization will come in very handy.

Value doesn't have to come from formal work experience. Are you a new dad? If your organization sells consumer products, share insights about customers like you. Does your religious or charitable activity give you access to important and influential members of the community? Introduce your teammates to them.

Think about all your experiences and relationships and how they might connect to the work of your team.

Life experience. The experiences that have shaped you are probably so central to who you are that you don't think about their value to your team. I realized that during an executive development session my colleague Tammy and I did with the top 70 leaders of a large hospital. Given the very personal nature of the program, we decided to start with introductions, even though many of the people in the room had worked together for years. Something very interesting happened. When the participants introduced themselves, they chose to comment on experiences that had shaped them as leaders.

One had learned tremendous discipline as a dancer. One was an Olympic athlete, and another ran ultramarathons (100 miles!). They all had great insight into endurance and stamina. Some had worked in other industries; at least one had spent time in politics, which could help the team understand the perspectives that shape public policy. And yet most of them hadn't talked about these amazing backgrounds with their colleagues. Their team didn't have access to the richness of their experience. Those experiences might not have added to their medical knowledge, but they certainly shed light on compassion, resilience, and stakeholder management.

All of You

Adding value is about more than just what you know and what you've done; it's also about how you see the world. Pretty much everything about you is relevant here. Think of any personality test you've ever taken. What did you learn about yourself? Are you an introvert or an extrovert? Are you more people-focused or task-focused? If you haven't taken a personality test, have you done one of those quizzes in *Cosmo* or *GQ*? Are you the risk taker or Mr. Play it Safe? Failing that, how does your family describe you? *"Bobby has always been our funny man. He can get us laughing in the darkest moments." "Betty is our planner. She has every summer vacation organized and booked by January!"* Somewhere, somehow, you've learned about your best qualities. Bring those great qualities to work with you. They will be valuable to your team.

Teams need diversity to be effective (I'll talk a lot more about this in Chapter 11). How do you enhance the diversity of your team? Maybe you tend to focus on the practical operations side, and your teammates are more strategic thinkers. Maybe you are more of a risk taker—many teams need someone to say that something is possible, or they'll never try anything new. Maybe your empathy helps you anticipate the impact of decisions—you may be able to help your team members influence the rest of the company more effectively. These are important perspectives you can bring to your team.

A word of warning: Your view of the world is both an asset and a liability. *You need to understand your biases* so that you'll know when they might be clouding your judgment or keeping you stuck in a certain way of looking at things.

The Naïve Question

Don't think that you have to have all the answers to add value. Sometimes the best way to help your team is to ask a really good question. Not a leading, phony, know-the-answer-before-you-ask question; a real, honest-to-goodness question. Curiosity is in short supply on many teams. We are so busy driving for the solution that we miss opportunities to understand why things work the way they do. The more you understand how something works or why it happens the way it does, the more likely you are to be able to steer things in the direction you want.

If your team tends to make a lot of assumptions, you can add value by asking questions. *"What causes people to act that way?" "How would the outcome be different if we tried a new approach?" "Who are we failing to mention in our analysis of the situation?"* Even if there is only a vague, niggling feeling in your gut, you can do your team a big favor by asking a question that pushes you to explore a little further.

A WORD ABOUT VULNERABILITY

It's pretty easy to add value when you know you're right, or at least when you know you have the expertise to weigh in on an issue. It's much harder to wade into a conversation when you aren't the expert and you're afraid your opinion might rub people the wrong way. All I can say is that those are the moments when you can add the most value.

Think about it. The least valuable contribution to your team is the one that's already been made. The person who persists in looking at a problem the same way as the last time (and the time before that) isn't making your team any more effective. But coming at the problem from a totally different angle, now *that's* useful! If only more people in meetings would ask themselves whether the comment they're about to make is going to add any new value before they started speaking.

Adding value, particularly adding value that is really novel, can be risky, but it's worth it. There are ways to introduce a different point of view that will increase the likelihood your teammates will listen and think about your input.

> *Set up your statement.* "*I feel like we need to explore this from a totally different perspective.*" That will cue your teammates to expect something different and not be caught off guard.

> *Make it clear what value you are trying to add.* "*I'm thinking about our customers who are senior citizens.*" That way, if you don't make the perfect point, they'll at least know what you're getting at.

> *Use questions instead of definitive statements.* "*We keep trying to make our dashboard in the new model slicker and sexier, but 30 percent of our customers are senior citizens. How might our new design affect them?*" Your teammates will be more likely to entertain a new idea without getting defensive if it comes in the form of a question.

Acknowledge attempts to think differently. *"I think Jack is on to something with the eyesight issue."* Just the fact that they were willing to play with your idea is a good sign. You want to encourage it.

Hand off the baton. *"Who's going to make sure we keep senior citizens in mind as we continue the design process?"* The last thing you want is for the issue to be seen as your issue. Instead, make it the team's issue.

Even if you're introducing new or unpopular ideas to the discussion, this approach will help make your ideas more palatable. There's no way to completely remove the risk of bringing up a new idea. Just focus on saying the things that need to be said and saying them in a way that your team will be comfortable hearing.

HOW DO I BREAK INTO THE INNER CIRCLE?

People often claim they can't add their full value because they aren't part of the team's so-called inner circle. What is fascinating is that the supposed members of this inner circle often don't see an inner circle, or, more important, they don't think there's an outer one.

But for those who see it, the inner circle is very real. The sense of being excluded from an in-group can be very demotivating. This dynamic can destroy what might otherwise have been a successful team.

What do you do if you're trapped outside the circle? Admission to the inner circle is decided more by the outsiders than the insiders. If you feel like you're on the outside, consider the following:

Have I connected with the people in the inner circle? Usually outsiders keep at a distance instead of engaging with the rest of the team. This is true both for work interactions and for lunch or other breaks. If you keep your distance, members of the inner circle will assume you aren't interested in joining. Step into the circle.

Am I working as hard as those people? Sometimes the inner circle forms among a group of people who work longer hours and go the extra mile. These people have learned to count on one another to get things done when it really matters. Next time a project requires extra hours, roll up your sleeves and find a way to be useful. Pitch in.

Do I have something valuable to offer? The inner circle, like the Justice League, needs diverse skills to be strong. If you've got a superpower they don't have (think Aquaman for undersea crime), offer it up. If members of the inner circle don't know what you can do, they won't seek you out. Be different.

Last, ask yourself whether the inner circle really exists, or whether it's a figment of your self-deprecating imagination. If you act like there's a wall between you and other members of your team, there might as well be. I can't tell you the number of times I've seen new people wander right into the inner circle while the others just stand watching from a distance. Which one will you be?

ADDING THE WRONG VALUE

If you feel like you're contributing and adding value on your team, there is one more question to ask yourself: Are you adding the right value? Here are some common ways you might be adding the wrong value on your team:

Too low. Sometimes you might add value that is below the level that is most useful. Micromanagement is a great example. Another would be getting into too much detail too soon in a process. When the value you're trying to add is at too low a level, people start to see you as irrelevant or controlling. If you think you're guilty of this, try answering more of the "what" and "why" questions and fewer of the "how" questions. You can even enlist a teammate to help you. Ask them to pick up their pen as a signal if you start getting into the weeds.

Too high. Another common problem is always flying at 40,000 feet. You need to make sure your big ideas are actually grounded in reality. If your ideas are too long-term, you need to focus on a more modest goal and a shorter time horizon. If your plans have only two points in them—like (1) start now, (2) reach a billion dollars in sales— you need to flesh out more details of how you will get from here to there. Your teammates can help you with this, too. Ask a friend on the team to give you a cue every time you sound like a dreamer. Maybe every time you throw out an amazing, visionary, ludicrous idea, they can respond with an emphatic *"Awesome!"* No one will know that's your signal to bring it back down out of the stratosphere.

Stepping on toes. Another dangerous mistake people make is to regularly add the value that someone else on the team is supposed to be adding. That's a good way to make enemies or be seen as a goody-two-shoes. No one likes being beaten to the punch in their own area of expertise, so don't put your teammate in that position. If you feel like a teammate isn't covering their bases, ask them to weigh in. *"This conversation is making me think about how this will play out when the new regulations come into place. Janet, what are some of the implications you're anticipating so far?"* If Janet comes back with, *"I hadn't thought of that, what is coming to mind for you?"* then you're at liberty to give your thoughts. If you leave room for your teammates to add value where they're supposed to, you won't mask any incompetence issues that should be addressed.

Broken record. In my third year of college, I lived in the basement of a house that backed onto a railroad track. The first few times the train went by and blasted its horn in the night, I sat bolt upright in bed, my heart pounding and my stomach in my throat—*what was that?* But as anyone who has lived in a situation like this knows, it wasn't long before I didn't even notice the train anymore. It was just background noise, like my roommate's TV and the old guy upstairs learning to play violin (okay, that was harder to block out). We have an incredible ability to get used to even the most overpowering sounds.

So here's the question to ask yourself: Are you the train on your team? Have you gone down that track so many times that people don't even hear you anymore? If you add the same value all the time, people will stop hearing you. If you feel like you are always the one who chimes in on a particular subject, try asking your teammates to play that role for a while. *"Even I'm getting sick of hearing myself talk about the budget. Who would be willing to think about the budget implications of this project?"* A new voice with the same message will be more likely to get through.

You never know where you will be able to add value when you show up as your whole self. But you are more than a supply chain manager, an accountant, or a digital marketer. You are an amazing amalgam of skills, experiences, relationships, and characteristics that are as unique as your fingerprint. Your team deserves all of that.

If you change the value you bring to the table, you'll change your team.

HEALTH CHECK: ARE YOU ADDING YOUR FULL VALUE?

If you turned off the autopilot and started to live up to your responsibility to Add Your Full Value, you should be contributing in the different ways detailed in the test in Figure 10.1. See how it adds up.

Responsibilities		Yes
Technical Expertise	I stay engaged in the discussion with my team.	☐
	I contribute fully in areas that are part of my role on the team.	☐
	I make proactive recommendations and suggestions.	☐
	I discuss the connections to my area when teammates are sharing their ideas.	☐
	I keep up with the latest ideas in my area.	☐
Experience	I know which of my experiences are the most unique and valuable to my team.	☐
	I share knowledge I have gained from roles outside my organization.	☐
	I comment on my insights about how stakeholders will perceive ideas.	☐
	I call on experiences I've had outside of work to broaden our thinking.	☐
	I ask questions when I don't have direct experiences to share.	☐
All of You	I use my relationships with colleagues and friends to benefit the team.	☐
	I have done some soul searching to understand my unique value.	☐
	I understand how I see the world differently than my teammates.	☐
	I make an extra effort to participate when my perspective is different.	☐
	I understand the informal role I play that helps my team be stronger.	☐
Not the Wrong Value	I stop and think about whether my comments are valuable before speaking.	☐
	I avoid getting into too much detail when the time isn't right.	☐
	I make sure that I ground my big ideas in reality.	☐
	I avoid adding value that someone else on the team should be adding.	☐
	I make sure that my contributions aren't predictable and repetitive.	☐

Figure 10.1 Add Your Full Value Health Check Test

YOUR RESPONSIBILITY IN REVIEW

1. It's easy to get in a rut of only contributing what you need to in order to get by.

   - You are exhausted by the overwhelming workload.

   - It's tempting to cope by becoming overly focused on your own component of the work while detaching from what is going on in the rest of the team.

   - Even when you try to contribute, you can have negative experiences that make it seem better to just mind your own business.

2. You need to add your full value.

   - Add your *technical value* by being proactive, by covering your angle even when discussions don't seem directly relevant, and by staying current in your area of expertise.

   - Use your *experience* from other companies, other departments, and other projects to bring insights that others on your team don't have.

   - Capitalize on *life experiences and relationships* from outside of work that could be valuable to your team.

   - Let your unique *personality* shine through by sharing your way of looking at the world with your teammates.

   - Ask great *naïve questions* to encourage your teammates to look at issues from different perspectives.

3. Be sure you're adding the right value.

   - Don't micromanage by adding value at *too low* a level. Avoid being tactical too soon or getting into the minutiae.

   - Don't be flighty by adding value at *too high* a level. Avoid being vague or delusional about what is possible.

(continued)

(continued)

- Don't *step on toes* by adding value that someone else on your team should be adding.

- Don't become the *broken record* by always adding value on the same topics or from the same perspective.

CHAPTER 11

Amplify Other Voices

The head of a small design consulting firm called me to talk about his team. They were a good group, he said, but they were having a few issues with the Controller. He was a staunch defender of the firm and a key person in making the place run, but the other members of the team found him tough to deal with. He caused a lot of conflict, and the team leader wasn't sure what to do about it. The good news was that he was willing to invest in making the team stronger.

As part of the process, we asked the members of the team to complete an assessment—one of the tools that uses colors to describe different styles.[1] Every once in a while, the assessment report tells the entire story of a team. This was one of those times. Five members of the team (the ones who were consultants) clung to the right-hand side of the grid. They were the big-ideas people. And there, out in the wilderness on the bottom left corner of the grid, the home of the processes-minded, sat one lone dot. Guess who—the Controller.

This mismatch made the team dynamic really tense. They spent most of their time talking about inspiring, innovative programs that would differentiate their firm and provide the kinds of solutions that their clients needed. Unfortunately, they spent almost no time talking about the realities of the budget or the expectations of the parent company in Europe. They left those issues to the Controller to manage. The team had settled into a dangerous habit of pigeon-holing him as the *bean counter* (you have to read that with a disdainful tone for full effect). They saw his opinion as something to be tolerated or worked around, rather than as a critical reality check for their overexuberance. And the more the team ignored him, the more cutting, sarcastic comments he made.

At our session, when I put the assessment grid on the screen, everyone got quiet. The controller could finally see in Technicolor what he had felt for years—one of these things is not like the others. The team knew immediately they needed to take ownership of the friction they had been feeling. It wasn't the controller who was the problem; it was the rest of the team who had been trying to drown out his voice.

The team dynamic changed immediately. Instead of trying to silence him or work around him, they started making space for the lone voice that was keeping the machine running. They sought out his opinion instead of ignoring it. It was amazing to see how relieved they all were. Now they would all be responsible for making room in the conversation for the controller and for weighing his opinions a little more seriously because he was the only one speaking from that perspective. It made a world of difference.

THE NEED FOR SPEED

Our productivity-crazed society tends to race from one thing to the next with the only goal being to go fast. We hardly ever stop to think whether it actually makes sense to go from Point A to Point B at all. Do you measure yourself on how far and how fast you've traveled rather than on the value of your destination?

Many organizations want their culture to have what they call a bias to action. A client of mine has the perfect comeback to this line: *"The greatest example of a bias to action is a hamster on a wheel—is that what you're going for?"* Sadly, lots of organizations are hamsters on wheels just running to get nowhere. Not something to strive for.

It's great when your team lets you go fast. When you trust one another, you go fast. When you are aligned, you go fast. When you ignore contradictory facts, you go fast. *Wait! Hold on a minute!* Couldn't sneak that past you? It really is that bad. If you're like most people, you don't like situations, or people, that slow you down, even when slowing down is exactly what you need to do to perform your job well. You like it when everybody just nods and agrees, because then you can go fast.

It's one thing to act decisively after considering all the facts, but it's another to do a shoddy job of collecting information and then conclude that the facts are in your favor. The need to speed things up can be justified. You don't need to go artificially slowly. But you can't go recklessly fast. You have to make room for the important stuff.

DROWNING OUT MINORITY VOICES—THE POWER AND THE PERIL OF THE MAJORITY

Teams are put together for many different reasons. How was your team formed? Was it a hand-selected group or a haphazard collection of the people who happened to be in certain roles? Lots of organizations just automatically consider people with similar roles a team. Teams are made up of several people with similar technical backgrounds and a single member from each of the supporting functions, like a business unit management team with the leaders for the Eastern, Central, Southern, and Western Regions, supported by the heads of finance and marketing. That skewed team is likely to have a lot of tactical and operational discussions, with moments of conflict between the one "great in theory" marketing representative and the four "get it done" regional leaders.

Imagine the conversation: *"We're rolling out a new store design for the spring season, so I've sent you the floor plans and the stock requirements,"* the marketing lead says enthusiastically.

"New store design! You've got to be kidding me, we just rolled out a new store design in January," the Southern Region lead complains loudly.

What happens next determines the health of the team. Unfortunately, more often than not, the majority jumps on the bandwagon and shuts down the conversation. *"No way, I'm not doing it,"* says the Western leader. The marketing lead tries to explain the rationale, but before he can get a word in edgewise, the Eastern leader puts the final nail in the coffin: *"You need to tell your friends at the head office that we can only do two redesigns a year."* The chorus responds in unison: *"No change in April."*

Corporate versus line, old guard versus new guard, one legacy organization in a merger versus the other—teams have majorities and minorities on all manner of different dimensions. Any team with a majority and a minority is set up for a biased conversation and a rocky dynamic. If the balance tips too far, you risk bad decision making and poor execution. A strong majority and a silent minority can lead to a Spectator team. If a strong majority overwhelms a powerless minority, it can create a Bobble Head team, where the minority just capitulates and goes along for the ride.

The majority versus minority dimension isn't always about roles. Your team could have a perfect balance of roles representing different parts of the organization, but the human beings filling the roles might be skewed in one way or another. If your team has a majority of extroverts, you're particularly susceptible to drowning out minority voices because those voices are quiet to begin with. The problem is especially worrisome because the introverts are the ones who are thinking while the extroverts are busy talking. You want to know what's going on in their heads, really you do!

Think about the personality variables measured by the different assessment tools. Are the majority of your team members concrete thinkers? If so, who's paying attention to the big picture? Are you much more task focused than people focused? Who's worrying about how the brilliant plan will be received by the troops? Is your team mostly risk takers with only one person who pays attention to what could go wrong?

Our whole society is based on the concept of one person, one vote. That system tells us that the majority is right; or more accurately, it tells us that the majority rules. We are so wedded to the concept that we make the mistake of thinking that majority rule is the way to run a team: "All in favor say *aye*."

But teams are not supposed to be democracies. Teams exist to move things forward, to make good decisions, to execute on strategy. The tyranny of the majority can make it very difficult to create meaningful progress. We need an alternative to majority rule. We need to give clout to the minority voices, not just the majority ones.

THE IMPORTANCE OF DIVERSITY

You need to hear and value the minority because diversity is critical to your team. Let me start by defining what I mean when I say *diversity*. That term has more baggage than my minivan on a summer road trip.

Over the past few years, the need to reduce systemic barriers to women, people of different races or cultural groups, and people with disabilities has brought tremendous attention to the topic of diversity. Unfortunately, it's made us think very superficially about what diversity is. People of different genders or skin colors don't always think differently. I live in the world's most multicultural city. I have the good fortune to work with people from all over the globe. Yet I've often found that a Harvard MBA–trained investment banker who is brown and was raised in India thinks a lot like a Harvard MBA–trained investment banker who is white and was raised in Connecticut. Gender and cultural diversity will increase your chances of having diversity of thought—but you can't assume it's enough. Your team needs diversity in the sense of different perspectives and points of view.

Diverse perspectives serve many important functions. We all tend to see the world through our own particular frame. It's like you look at the world through your office window and what you can see from there is all that exists. Everybody has their windows. If you have always worked in the United States, your view of the customer, of the market, and of employees will be constrained. If you are an accountant, that will influence how you see a situation. Your contribution will be limited by the frame you're looking through.

Seeing opportunity. Depending on your frame, you will see different opportunities for your business. The narrower your frame, the fewer opportunities you will see. For example, teams trying to build a better portable music player through better hardware couldn't compete with the Apple team, who saw the opportunity through the frame of hardware, software, licensing, and more.

Likewise, bankers were limited by thinking of a bank branch as a place to conduct efficient private transactions. They needed the inspiration of retail experts who could see the opportunity to convert branches into stores. Instead of walled-off offices that leave financial products a mystery to most of us, they saw the potential to open up the space and let customers see and touch the whole line of products. This helped banks convert more banking customers into investment clients or insurance policyholders.

There is no way to have all these broad perspectives in one person. But when your team brings together a more complete view of the world, the opportunities are endless.

Spotting threats. Diversity also helps your team see threats in the environment. You are probably hypersensitive to the types of risks that have affected you in the past—humans are pretty darn good at learning from things that went disastrously wrong. Unfortunately, you're probably pretty bad at anticipating problems that haven't happened yet. I am very fond of the old military adage that "generals are always preparing for the last war."

Because people from different industries, backgrounds, or disciplines pay attention to different factors in the environment, when you bring their perspectives into your team, you can cover more ground when scanning for concerns.

Leveraging strengths. Our industrial folklore is full of stories about teams of people seeing possibility in things that others thought were useless. Legendary among them is the story of the origin of 3M's Post-it Note, from chemist Dr. Spencer Silver's failed attempt at superglue combined with Art Fry's need for something to keep his bookmarks from falling out of his hymnbook. The result was a repositionable, tacky paper that transformed the value of a notepad. Interestingly, 3M had the glue for nine years before a person with a different perspective saw a way to use it. This story is also a good reminder of a lesson from Chapter 10: Activities outside of work (in this case, singing in the church choir) can help you add your full value.

Mitigating weaknesses. It's great when diversity on a team helps you capitalize on strengths, but sometimes you need diverse points of view to compensate for your weaknesses. One of history's most famous examples of this is the team at NASA Mission Control that found a way to repair the Apollo 13 spaceship well enough for it to hobble back to Earth. Any team that needs to accomplish goals with few resources should take an afternoon to watch the movie about that harrowing event. The resourcefulness and creative thinking of the Mission Control team who cobbled together an adapter that gave the crew enough oxygen to make the trip home safely is truly inspiring.

To be strong, innovative, and protected from risk, your team needs to be able to see the world from different angles: from inside the box, outside the box, above the box, below the box. You especially need people who don't even see the box! If your team doesn't have that kind of diversity, you are at a serious disadvantage.

Here's the challenge: Diversity of thought slows you down. At least, it feels like it slows you down. In reality, without diversity you might rocket through decision making only to grind to a halt during implementation. When you slow down to incorporate different perspectives early on, you actually come out ahead in the end. But most teams feel such a compulsion to move fast, to get somewhere even if that somewhere doesn't make sense, that they ignore or shut down any voice that slows them down.

AMPLIFY OTHER VOICES

In rare instances, teams have a member whose views are in the minority, but who has enough confidence and courage to raise unpopular opinions proudly. This was the role Richard Feynman played in the Rogers Commission's investigation of the causes of the space shuttle *Challenger* explosion. Everyone else on the 14-member commission was willing to let NASA downplay the issues behind the disaster and handle their problems internally, so Feynman had to protest loudly to get his minority report included in the commission findings. His report exposed the terrible breakdowns in communication, systemic mis-representation of risks, and wildly flawed decision making that led to the shuttle exploding shortly after liftoff. Without his dogged determination to get to the bottom of the issue, the vulnerability of the O-rings in the shuttle's booster rockets might never have come to light—putting future missions and crews in jeopardy.

If you agree that diversity is critical to teams, then you need to make more room for minority voices. You might argue that these people should do what it takes to get a word in edgewise, like Richard Feynman did. But let's consider that idea for a moment. Richard Feynman was a Nobel Prize–winning physicist. He was voted one of the top 10 physicists of all time for his contributions to quantum physics and nanotechnology. He was not an average guy. Even with his extraordinary talents, many people in the shuttle investigation tried to silence him. Now imagine a mere mortal trying to stand up against opposing voices.

You can't count on someone on your team having the chutzpah to do what Feynman did. It is very difficult to be heard over a choir of voices. It's hard to be the one who has to disagree. It's even harder to repeat the same concerns multiple times if your team members don't hear you right away. It's so hard, so unpleasant, that you can't count on your teammates to do it.

Instead, when you are in the majority, you have to make sure that minority perspectives are heard and considered. You need to Amplify Other Voices. You need to lend your credibility to those

who are struggling to be heard. It's much easier for you to help bring attention to a different perspective than for one person to do it alone.

Give Them the Floor

The first thing you need to do is to create space for other perspectives to be shared. That means you need to make room for them in the conversation. This sounds easy, but it actually takes a significant amount of attention to participate in the meeting and observe it at the same time. Who is speaking and who is not? Which perspectives are monopolizing the conversation? If you are participating very actively, you might not notice these dynamics. It's easy to get to the end of a meeting before you realize that you didn't hear from one of the members of the team.

In addition to listening well, you need to observe body language and nonverbal reactions. Even if your team member doesn't express his thoughts directly, you can probably tell that he disagrees or is uncomfortable. Instead of talking about his concerns, he communicates through rolling eyes, withdrawn eye contact, or defensive and closed body language.

Your job is to interject and invite that teammate to share his point of view. The most generic version of that is as follows: "*Henry, we haven't heard your perspective on this issue yet. What are you thinking as we're talking?*" If you know specifically what value your teammate could add, call it out. "*Maria, we often forget to think about our Latin American customers. How do you think this would go over with them?*" You can also make it easier for someone to provide a contrasting opinion by showing that you welcome it. "*John, I'm starting to worry that we're getting caught up in sunshine and rainbows here. What risks are we ignoring?*" Imagine how much easier it would be to share a contrary or even critical opinion when you've specifically been asked to do so. This is one way to make room for diversity.

Defend against Silencing

Making room for a teammate with an unpopular perspective is really important. Unfortunately, it's not usually enough. Often, even when the minority has voiced its opinion, concerns, or criticism, the team doesn't really hear them. If six voices have all endorsed a plan, one voice suggesting that the team proceed with caution might not slow down the charge. You will probably need to run interference for your teammate.

The first thing to guard against is the mindless brush-off. These are the comments that make it seem as though the team has listened, considered, and chosen to ignore a dissenting point of view when really they just don't want to be bothered taking it in. A comment such as "Yeah, yeah, we got that" is a great example of the brush-off. You can counteract the brush-off with a question that requires your teammates to actually work with the information. "*Bupinder is talking about the risk that our servers won't be able to handle that load. What tests have we done on different load scenarios?*"

The second thing to watch for is the "not-applicable" defense. In this case, your team members provide reasons why the issue being raised is irrelevant. There are different forms of the not-applicable defense, but the most common is when someone says, "*We've tried that before and it didn't work.*" In that case, you can keep the issue open by asking, *"What might have changed in our business that would make the outcome different this time?"* Minimizing ideas or passing them off as highly improbable are also examples of the not-applicable defense. In this case, you can encourage the team to think the issue through before moving on. *"That scenario might be unlikely, but how would it affect our plan if by chance it did happen?"* If your teammates try to minimize the impact of a comment, use questions to force them to process the information more thoroughly.

The third and most devastating way that teams shut down minority voices is by using humor to trivialize the issue or to belittle the person who raised it. Bleeding Back teams with strong passive-aggressive cultures often use sarcasm to cut down a person with a troubling perspective. For example, in a consumer packaged-goods company, potential retailer concerns about new packaging could be very serious. But if the marketer on the team is wedded to his new design, he might deflect the issue by making the salesperson look wimpy or like he's kowtowing to the stores. *"Right, I forgot that the stores should be making decisions about how we brand our products. Silly me."*

If someone's using humor to deflect a real issue, you really need to rescue your teammate. But it's tricky to do this well. If you're too quick to jump in or if you come across as chastising your sarcastic teammate, you'll probably get lumped in with the victim and you'll both be useless. Instead, let the laugh happen and then gently bring the issue back up. *"That's pretty funny and we certainly wouldn't want that. At the same time, we have to think about whether this packaging is going to make it hard to sell our product. We sure don't want them cursing us while we're trying to negotiate for prime shelf space. What do we think the big three chains are going to say?"* If you demonstrate that humor won't work as a technique for silencing the issue, your teammates will learn not to try it in the first place.

Use the Agenda

On your team, are minority perspectives intentionally or inadvertently silenced by positioning them at the very end of the agenda?

In many team meetings, nobody's watching the clock, and items well down the agenda never get covered. Or if they do, it's often when there is little time for proper discussion and little energy to address the issue thoroughly. When you notice this happening, you need to lobby for changes to the agenda. *"I've noticed that we often miss the section of the agenda on talent planning. Could we move that to the top of the agenda for our next meeting?"*

If you are a team leader, you can use the formal structure of the meeting to support the diversity cause. If you think an agenda item might be minimized, assign a different member of the team to chair that portion of the meeting. Make it clear that you're counting on her to create a full discussion on the subject, regardless of her personal views. This technique borrows from the old high school English teacher trick of asking you to debate the opposite side of a resolution that you support. If you want a good grade, you have to come up with some clever arguments against your own thinking. Brilliant!

Here's the ultimate test. Your responsibility to amplify other voices doesn't just apply when you think those minority voices have a good point. In fact, your responsibility is really put to the test when someone holds an opinion you disagree with. It's even more important when you react viscerally to their point of view. It's those situations that test how committed you are to a healthy team. Don't pretend that you agree, just make sure that you create room for the other point of view. *"Wow, I'm really uncomfortable with that idea. Can we take one step back? You're going to have to help me understand the implications of what you're saying."* When you can make room for an opinion that frustrates you, angers you, or even hurts you, you are really earning your spot on the team.

What If the Voice Isn't There?

Sometimes, the minority voice that you need to hear just isn't on your team. Is your team so skewed that important perspectives are completely missing? The missing element can be a certain function within your organization. Maybe your team has no representative from marketing or from the field. It can also be a stakeholder group that isn't represented well, as is the case on teams with no customer advocate or no voice of suppliers or distributors. Or it could be a style that you're missing. Maybe no one pays attention to detail or thinks creatively about options. When a voice is missing from the team, you can't amplify it.

When that's the case, you need to use other tactics to get the viewpoint included in the discussion. You can invite guests to the table to have them talk about a particular topic. Hosting them in person can be very valuable as it gives you a chance to poke and prod and really understand the issue from their perspective. Just don't poke too hard or they might not come back!

If you can't get a different perspective straight from the horse's mouth, you can still broaden your thinking. You can assign a certain perspective to a member of your team and ask that they chime in with ideas or concerns as they listen to the discussion. I worked with a brand team at an appliance manufacturer to help them think through the customer perspective. The target customer was a working mother in her thirties or forties, but the brand team was mostly composed of young men in their twenties. We conducted a session all about the customer's typical day. We had them feeding and dressing a screaming kid, getting themselves dressed in heels and pearls while singing "The Wheels on the Bus" to placate the child (a mental image I will never forget), and grocery shopping in a store that kept changing its layout to make sure they travelled through more aisles and bought more products. Suddenly they had a much more realistic perspective on what features in the dishwasher, fridge, and washing machine would and wouldn't be attractive to their customer.

Another team had a fun and creative way to remind itself about its deficit in the action orientation category. They had learned through their assessment that the team had no members with "red" styles. Red is the color associated with being decisive and achieving tangible results. Because the team had no easy way of bringing in a member with this style, they put a red teddy bear on their meeting table. The teddy bear reminded them that they needed to take an action log at the end of every meeting and assign each item an owner and date by which it needed to be completed. Red Bear also reminded them to start their meetings with follow-up to ensure the items had been addressed. If you are missing a perspective on your team, you can use small, tangible things to remind you to approach issues from multiple angles.

WHAT IS DIVERSE?

What are the dimensions on which your team needs better balance? There are really too many to name each individually. In fact, as the market changes and evolves, new perspectives become valuable all the time. There is no way to represent every possible perspective, but there are a few general categories to which you need to pay attention.

Functions and roles. Modern organizations divide work into categories to foster technical excellence and increase efficiency. This makes a lot of sense. The downside is that teams with very narrow mandates can become silos, isolated and insulated from the rest of the organization. No matter what role your team plays, spend some time thinking about the other parts of your organization and how they'd react to your ideas and decisions. Think about different departments, different product lines, corporate functions like IT, finance, HR, marketing—what would their voices add to your discussions?

Stakeholders. Another set of critical perspectives for your team comes from outside of your organization. Your team should be able to draw on the perspectives of key stakeholders such as your customers, clients, industry partners, suppliers, distributors, regulators, and community leaders. This is by no means an exhaustive list, but it gives you an idea of how many different points of view you need to consider. With stakeholders, you don't necessarily need to physically bring people from outside your organization in to your team (although that can be useful at times); you just need to ensure that there are people on the team thinking about and raising issues from those perspectives during the normal course of your discussions.

Thinking styles. The final major category of perspectives that need to be represented on your team can be labeled broadly as thinking styles. These are the different ways that you and your teammates experience and process information in the world around you. Different people will respond to the same situation in entirely different ways, and your team is at its strongest when you can capitalize on this fact. You need people who can see the big picture and the connections between things that allow you to build a strong plan. You also need people who can see the fine detail and the small nuances that will change how successfully a plan is implemented. You need to balance the task at hand with the impact on people, to listen both to the aversion to risks and the benefits of taking them.

Diverse voices are hard to listen to because they stop you in your tracks and make you think differently, usually more deeply. That's uncomfortable. So, if you're like most people with the power of the majority behind you, you will probably blow off those minority points of view. If you aren't completely confident in your position in the majority, you might silence the minority by undermining your teammate's credibility. But just as it's deadly for a body to reject a donor organ, it is foolish to drown out the minority voice on your team. Your team needs diverse perspectives to support healthy decision making. If you're in the majority, it's your responsibility to make room for them to emerge.

If you change how you respond to the minority, you'll change your team.

HEALTH CHECK: ARE YOU AMPLIFYING OTHER VOICES?

If you have taken your responsibility to Amplify Other Voices seriously, you should be able to check off the items in the test in Figure 11.1 with a clear conscience. How are you doing?

Responsibilities		Yes
Give Them the Floor	I pay attention to how people are participating in the team.	☐
	I notice when people or perspectives get shut down in the discussion.	☐
	I refrain from talking too much if others haven't had a chance to contribute.	☐
	I invite my teammates who aren't contributing to join in the discussion.	☐
	I ask for people to contribute perspectives that seem to be missing.	☐
Defend against Stifling	I notice when a teammate is being brushed off.	☐
	I talk about the importance of considering minority perspectives.	☐
	I ask questions to encourage my teammates to think more deeply.	☐
	I reintroduce ideas that get passed over too quickly.	☐
	I call it out when my teammates use humor to shut someone down.	☐
Use the Agenda	I retain my energy and interest for items late in the agenda.	☐
	I encourage the team to make room for all agenda items.	☐
	I offer to lead discussions on less popular agenda topics.	☐
	I ask to rotate the order of items that often get missed.	☐
	I ask for more time on issues that don't get addressed fully.	☐
Defend the Dissenter	I am aware when I react negatively to an issue raised by a teammate.	☐
	I am upfront about how issues are affecting me.	☐
	I keep my mind open to the value of ideas that make me uncomfortable.	☐
	I ask questions to understand opinions that I don't agree with.	☐
	I ask my teammates to give unpopular opinions a full airing.	☐

Figure 11.1 Amplify Other Voices Health Check Test

YOUR RESPONSIBILITY IN REVIEW

1. The desire to move fast can cause you to shut down diverse perspectives.

   - Members of the majority have strength in numbers, but the most common point of view is not always the correct one.

   - Diversity is critically important in identifying opportunities, mitigating risks, capitalizing on strengths, and overcoming weaknesses.

2. You need to amplify other voices on your team.

   - Make room for minority points of view in the conversation. When they are being shut out, *give them the floor*.

   - Defend against attempts to brush off or belittle minority voices. *Don't let those voices be silenced*.

   - Recommend changes to the *agenda* if certain items are frequently missed or rushed.

   - Find creative ways to bring in voices or perspectives that are *missing from the team*.

3. Increase diversity on critical dimensions.

   - Represent different *functions and roles* from across your organization.

   - Bring in the voices of *external stakeholders* such as customers, distributors, and the communities in which you do business.

   - Respect the contribution of different *personalities and thinking styles* to bring insights to issues and opportunities.

CHAPTER 12

Know When to Say "No"

The leadership team of an innovative healthcare company had assembled in a rustic old coach house nestled in the heart of the city. I remember the room vividly for two reasons. First, because we were talking about space-age technology while sitting in a 150-year-old garage. Second, because the sloping ceilings made it nearly impossible to post things on the walls. We were there to set the team's course for the coming year, and, given the overwhelming number of projects they were trying to accomplish, I really needed to stick things on the walls!

The team faced a problem many organizations would envy: They couldn't keep up with the demand for their services. They had introduced a new way of delivering healthcare that made high-quality care more accessible, cost effective, and timely. The problem now was that everyone wanted a piece of them and the small organization was straining under the load.

They came into the retreat with a list of 73 strategic projects for the next fiscal year. I gently explained that strategic planning is as much about what you're not going to do as what you are going to do. They listened and then set to work cutting their list—to 27 high-priority strategic initiatives.

Fabulous! We had progress—*I thought*. But when they presented their ideas, they hadn't taken anything off the table. Instead, they had played that old shell game of grouping projects under new, broader umbrella terms, without actually removing a single activity. Back to the drawing board.

The team defined the imperatives for their business in the coming year. These five statements were not actions or projects, but insights about what they needed to achieve to be successful. For example, one imperative was "solve key health system challenges" and another was "create a scalable approach." These imperatives created a lens through which to look at a proposed initiative. They allowed the team to evaluate projects based on how many imperatives they would advance—the more, the better.

Now they were ready to take another crack at the project list. I broke the group into pairs and assigned one imperative to each pair. Then I distributed the original list of 73 projects and asked each pair to review the list and select the projects that would create significant progress on their imperative. I was the only person in the room who wasn't surprised when 31 initiatives were left orphaned with no one claiming them as critical to the success of their imperative.

There were more battles getting that remaining list of 42 down to the 20 projects that eventually made the cut, but the war had been won when they finally understood that they wouldn't accomplish their ambitious goals if they continued to be all things to all people. They realized that in such a new organization, gaining more traction and building momentum with high-quality delivery would do more for everyone than trying to do too much and failing. They were too important to fail.

Spread Too Thin

The vast majority of workers today will never actually *finish* their work. The word *finished* is a relic of another era. Sure, you complete a task or a project, but when was the last time that you packed up your desk and felt like you had tied up the loose ends and finished what needed to be done? I can't remember a time. I bet you could work 24 hours a day, 7 days a week, 52 weeks a year and never get everything done.

Me too. I have a full-time job in a vibrant and growing consultancy. My role in selling work can never be done. It's not like there is a sales bucket to be filled and once it's done I can shut off the tap. Every salesperson is always looking for what's next. If I've finished following up with my existing clients, I can always call a new prospect. And that doesn't even begin to cover what social media has done to my world. I can finish writing this book, but I'll never finish writing my blog. And don't get me started on Twitter. Work itself is *unfinishable*. I take it as a given that you have more to do than is humanly possible.

So that's where you need to start. Your organization, your team, your boss all ask more of you than is humanly possible. But you are the one who says "yes." You need to think about why you say "yes" before you can start figuring out when and how you're going to say "no."

Fitting In

Chapter 5 explored the strength of the drive to affiliate. Humans are wired to connect with people, and we are compelled to do and say things that will help us do that. This makes most of us incredibly eager to be *in* and very afraid of being *out*. To make sure that you are part of the in-group, you say "yes" to things that aren't inherently valuable to you but instead are just evidence that you are important, valued, and part of the club.

My girlfriend Lisa nailed it for me. For one of our girls' night out events, we were going to a shop to make photo albums for our kids. She doesn't really like crafty activities and wasn't even prepared with the materials to do the project. She walked through the door and announced that she was there only because of a wicked case of FOMO: fear of missing out. I laughed so hard I nearly keeled over, mostly because that's the exact motivation for so many things I do. It's not because I want to be in on the activities; it's because I don't want to be kept out of them. What if the group hatched a new inside joke? What if they set a date for our next get-together and no one e-mailed me?

FOMO most certainly happens in our personal lives, but it's a significant problem on teams, too. Do you have FOMO problems on your team? How many meetings do you attend just to make sure you don't miss something? Could you send a delegate? Could you just catch up on the minutes after the meeting? It's not only about meetings; what projects do you sign up for because all the important people will be working on them? Are you deliberate about picking the ones that are really valuable and declining the ones that aren't? And when it comes to e-mail, FOMO is bringing us to our knees. People ask to be copied on the most inane messages just because they would hate to miss anything.

If your workload is at least partially attributable to things you're doing just to avoid missing out, you are going to need to get a handle on that before reading the rest of the chapter. If doing stuff and being involved is your ticket to self-esteem, it's going to be really painful when you have to start saying "no."

Pulling Your Weight

Maybe the descriptions of FOMO don't ring true for you. There's another reason why you might be saying "yes" to things that you shouldn't, and that's your own perception of what a good team player looks like. Most of us have internalized the idea that good team players say "yes" when they are asked to do something. *Really* good team players step up and volunteer without even being asked. When they do, we praise their initiative. We've socialized people to stretch themselves to the breaking point, all in service of "taking one for the team."

This is a really difficult thing to manage. If work is unfinishable but you want to leave the office at the end of the day, you are going to have to leave things incomplete. Now imagine that as you shut down your computer and put on your coat, Drew is sitting beside you working away. He looks harried. He's running his hands through his hair and sighing deeply. You might feel like you have to help him out. You might go grab a couple of coffees and switch your computer back on. If you're like me, you'll head home because there are people there who will notice if you're late, but you'll wait until everyone's asleep and log back in to help Drew then.

If Drew is working on the right things, this might actually be productive. If you're pulling your weight in a tug of war with the competition, that makes sense. But if you're pulling your weight by just dragging a big boulder of meaningless work around in circles, then you're wasting your time and energy. You need to get control of your own workload before you can rescue your teammates.

Life Is a Smorgasbord

There is one more common reason why you might agree to take on more work: You like it! It's not too difficult for you to understand that taking on tasks that you can't do well won't make you more valuable to your teammates. It's much more difficult to convince you not to take on work that you find interesting and rewarding. That's a huge challenge.

Are you feasting at the buffet of life? Many people take on new tasks the way some people approach a smorgasbord: They take a little bit of a lot of things because everything looks so yummy. Mmmm, mashed potatoes, gravy, Caesar salad, roast beef, wontons, egg rolls, pad Thai, tiramisu all on one plate. The only problem is that cramming a plate so full makes the gravy on the mashed potatoes spoil the salad and the salad dressing saturates the dessert. When you look at all you're trying to do at work, is there gravy on your salad?

If you're genuinely curious about the world, work can be a never-ending series of temptations. Adding a new responsibility to your job description would add variety and enrich your work. A new project would give you a chance to apply the skills you just learned in a training program. Working on the charity committee would allow you to give back on issues that matter. For the chronically fascinated person, these urges to explore and learn and grow can be counter-productive. If your plate is so full that you can't enjoy anything anymore, you need to curb your enthusiasm.

In my experience as a manager, I find people's compulsion to say "yes"—to fit in, to pull their weight, or to satisfy their curiosity—

is so strong that new employees will take on more and more work and stop only when they finally (and inevitably) drop the ball. The result is a difficult, embarrassing episode, which can have a devastating effect on the team. For a brief period of time, the person might avoid saying "yes" to a few things. But before long, the really keen team members are back to saying "yes" to everything.

Alarmingly, this tendency to take on more and more work doesn't lessen much even with time and experience. You are talented, aligned, and engaged, yet if you keep saying "yes" to too many things, the result will be teammates with chronically poor execution, little confidence in one another, and levels of stress and anxiety that make your whole team a powder keg waiting to blow.

The Role of Bad Leadership

It's not just you as an overeager team member who is to blame for unmanageable workloads. Your team leader needs to take responsibility for the role he plays, too. His failure to prioritize and make tough decisions about what is more—*and less*—important leaves you no alternative but to add something else to your already full plate.

Early in my career, I worked for a boss who left her employees in tears because she expected them to say "yes" to everything. One afternoon around 3:00, our executive assistant came to me in a terrible state. The boss had just dropped a pile of five items on her desk. Each item had a sticky note on it with the word "urgent." She told the boss that she had to leave at 4:30 for a medical appointment and asked that she prioritize the items so she could get to the most urgent. The boss just said they were "all urgent." The assistant told me that her husband was picking her up on the street outside our office tower and that she had no way to reach him to say she'd be late (this was before cell phones). She was frantic. She didn't want to let the boss down, but she couldn't leave her husband sitting in traffic. She did what she could before 4:30 and then left for her appointment.

No one on our team (except perhaps the boss) was surprised when she resigned three weeks later.

Often, part of the problem is that your team leader doesn't have the courage to manage up. You probably think of your boss as being pretty powerful and having a fair degree of control. But every team leader in an organization is a team member on their boss's team. Even the CEO reports to the board, and boards are notoriously guilty of coming up with time-sucking, impractical projects that get the whole organization spinning. Just as you worry about fitting in and pulling your weight, so does your boss. Just as you give in and add the additional work to your already packed calendar, so does your boss. She grudgingly accepts more and more work from above without asking for some to be removed or at least prioritized. If you are a leader and you're guilty of this, keep reading. It's time to get back in control.

KNOW WHEN TO SAY "NO"

We have reached the point where we think it's easier to say "yes" than to say "no." That's because we talk about decisions to take on work as if they are personal and independent. *"If I choose to take on more work, that's my own problem. I can deal with my angry spouse and cope with the stress and lack of sleep."* But if you think that way, you are grossly underestimating the effect that your workload has on your team.

If you fail to deliver because you took on too much, your team will lose confidence in you. Your mistakes may make other team-mates look foolish or irresponsible. If you rush through the work, the flaws in your piece will compromise the whole. If you spend too much time doing unimportant stuff and fail to get to the big things, the team will have to go without or make someone else cover for you. You have got to get over the idea that good team players say "yes." "Yes" drives you nuts, reduces your effectiveness, and results in poor-quality work. You have to Know When to Say "No."

Setting Your Criteria

The first step in the process of saying "no" is to determine which things you should be saying "yes" to. The vast majority of the work you take on should be right in your sweet spot: the intersection between what you were hired to do, what you are great at, and what is most important to your team in the current situation. Your goal is to find the overlap between those three circles and spend as much time and energy as you can working on those tasks.

It might be tempting to spend time working on things that fall outside that sweet spot, but it's not worth it. Even work that satisfies two of the three conditions is suboptimal compared with work that fits all three. Play out the different scenarios and you'll see the issues:

- If you were hired to do it and you're great at it, but it's not important to your team at the moment, then you're probably putting off doing something that's even more important.

You may feel good about doing meaningful work, but if it's not the most important work you could be doing, you can't afford it. Don't procrastinate.

- If you're great at it and it's important to the team, but it's not your role, you're doing someone else's job. If your boss chooses to change your job because you're better suited to this work, then it's a different story, but until then, don't spend time doing someone else's job when you have a job to get done yourself. Don't overstep.

- If you were hired to do the work and it's important to the team, but you're not great at it, you're in over your head. Tell your team you're not positioned to succeed. Ask for the help you need to do the job well. Maybe you need to work with someone who's done it before. Maybe you need extra coaching from your boss. Fumbling around with work you're not good at is not a good use of anyone's time. Don't pretend.

Once you know what type of work you should be doing, you can evaluate anything that comes along and get a sense of whether you should take it on. Even if you're gunning for a big promotion, master the job you have now first. Get really good at focusing and prioritization because those fundamentals will be essential if you want to move up in your organization.

When to Say "No"

During World War I, each machine gun had a three-man crew. Legend has it that a bright young recruit noticed that although two of the men were fully engaged, the third was just standing there a couple of paces back and to one side of the gun. When he asked what that man did, the answer was, "He used to hold the mule when the gun was fired." When they did away with the mule, apparently they forgot to do away with the mule holder, which begs the question: Are you holding an imaginary mule? Consider the following points before you cut tasks from your to-do list.

Not now, not ever. There are things that you just need to delete from your task list altogether—like holding the mule. They don't add value for you, for the team, or for your organization. It's surprising how many of these tasks actually exist. Most are remnants of previous eras and administrations. Probably some of them were relevant at some point but have outlived their usefulness.

A friend of mine was the VP of IT for a division of a large computer company. His people were constantly complaining that they were stretched too thin, that they didn't have time to add the value they wanted or to think proactively about the business. The culprit: a list of 18 monthly reports they had to send to the head office every month. My friend stopped sending one report each month until someone noticed. How many months do you think it took before anyone noticed? *Nine.* He deleted eight reports and freed his team up to focus on the things they really needed to be doing.

Not now, maybe later. Unfortunately, most tasks can't just be deleted. Fortunately, however, a lot of them can at least be delayed. This is the discipline of prioritization. You need to figure out which items are less important right now, decide when to reopen them, and then put them back on the agenda when the time comes. Great teams know that even the most brilliant plans can fall flat if attempted too soon. At the strategic level, you can delay because the customer isn't ready, because the organization won't yet buy in, or because you have a bigger opportunity to capitalize on first.

Delaying action can be strategic, but you can also do this pragmatically in your day-to-day work. For example, when people panic and overreact to new problems, they create crazy amounts of extra work. Instead of jumping in, wait for the flailing to stop and assess the situation before taking knee-jerk action.

I'm often reminded of this approach when I'm traveling on business and I pick up a day's worth of messages at the same time at the end of the day. I'll often get one message recorded in the morning that says "urgent" and asks me to do X, Y, and Z, and then another two hours later saying, *"No need to worry, we've handled it."* They got the job done and I didn't add to the mêlée by trying to get involved.

Not Quite "No"

The first couple of tactics for deleting work are based on the idea that the work isn't valuable, at least not right now. Many of the requests you get to take on new tasks will be for legitimate, important work that needs to get done. For those situations, there are other ways to manage your workload.

The first is the situation in which the work is important, but it's not in your sweet spot because it's a better fit with someone else's role or abilities. In that case, you need to get the work to the optimal person for the job. I face this one all the time. As a senior member of our consulting team, I'm one of the go-to people for meetings with new clients, especially if they've seen me give a keynote speech or read an article I've written. But I'm not always the best person to represent the team if the issue at hand falls outside of my expertise or the client's industry isn't one I know well. My team counts on me to pass these opportunities on to people who can do the work more effectively.

Other times when teammates approach me to do work, I might be able to do it, but it might be overkill. It's a great chance to delegate. If I take on an assignment that could be done well by a more junior person, I'm denying them a chance to spread their wings, I'm making the client pay more than they need to for the work, and I'm not focusing on the work that only I can do. That's a triple waste! This brings me to a very important distinction.

Add Unique Value

I try hard to make my own workload decisions with the idea of adding value in mind. Unfortunately, this filter has failed me and it will probably fail you too, if it hasn't already. It's just not stringent enough. If you're well along in your career, or if you're early in your career and smart as a whip, you can probably add value on most topics. As discussed in Chapter 10, if you're adding your full value, then no one is exactly like you because no one has your precise collection of knowledge, experiences, and characteristics. If Adding Your Full Value were enough, there wouldn't be a Chapter 12. You have to be more discerning; you have to differentiate between value and unique value.

You add unique value when you're in your sweet spot: doing important stuff that's part of your job and that you're the best at. If you're adding value that won't make a meaningful difference to the quality or success of the work, move along. If you are adding value that someone else is already able to add, you're redundant; get out of the way! I once saw a CEO jump into a debate about what should be in the gift basket for customers attending their conference. Yup, making millions and adding the same value as the marketing coordinator fresh out of business school. Stick to your unique value add.

Honey, I shrunk the work. Even when work is important and you are the right person to do it, you can still be disciplined and smart about how much time and energy it consumes. You should always be on the lookout for ways to pare work back to its core, without losing the essential elements. Figure out the intention of the activity and find ways to accomplish the goal with less effort.

This technique becomes increasingly important when you're collaborating with other teams. Because of the emphasis on collaboration and internal customer service, it's really hard to say "no." People outside your team will make requests without understanding the work required to fulfill them. To keep focused on the most important aspects of the task, ask questions. *"What are you trying to achieve?" "What can you do on your own and what do you need from me?" "The first five numbers you asked for are easy to get, but the sixth will take me a couple of days. Can you live without it?"*

Meetings offer a lot of opportunities to shrink your workload. How many meetings are you invited to only as a courtesy? Once it's clear that you won't add unique value, it's better for everyone if you make the tough choice to say "no" to that meeting. Imagine how many one-hour meetings could be half-hour meetings if there were fewer people present.

A final note about diminishing work: Think about what needs to be industrial strength and what can be fit for purpose. A client once made this distinction when talking about the level of investment in various functions of his company. To this day it's still one of the most helpful ways I've found of talking about effort and workload. Some companies have a quality culture so baked into their DNA that full-on is the only way they know how to do things. Some tasks need to be done full-on, industrial strength, but for others, good enough is good enough.

Several years ago, I worked with a group of nuclear physicists. If these brilliant people had one minor flaw, it was that they did everything with the rigor and control required for handling radioactive materials. That made things move a little slowly when it came to HR processes or building customer relationships. Ask yourself whether you need everything you do to be industrial strength or whether there are some things that just need to be fit for purpose.

How to Say "No"

Although this responsibility is called "Know When to Say 'No,'" it really should be when *and how* to say "no." You've probably heard someone say "no" in a way that makes you feel shut down or devalued, but there is a better way.

Here is how to say "no" without alienating people:

Question the work. Help your teammate go through the same thought process you went through to determine whether the work is necessary. Ask some good questions and listen to the answers with an open mind. For example, if someone asked you to attend an industry event that you don't feel is an effective use of your time, you might ask, *"Who is the target audience for the event?" "Are the people there potential buyers of our services?" "Where would this event fit in relative priority to the other three we are already sponsoring?"* Help your teammate figure out whether the work is worth doing at all.

If they come to the same conclusion as you, that it can be deleted, you're done. If not, go to the next step.

Tell them what you are saying "yes" to. If you have gone through a process to determine your priorities and define your sweet spot on the team, share that with them. If the things you're working on are clearly important and a good use of your time, it will be easier for your teammate to understand your reluctance. For example, if you had to turn down a new project opportunity, you could say, *"Thanks so much for thinking of me. This looks like fun work. Right now I've agreed with the team leader that my focus is on working with financial services companies and I feel like if I take this assignment, then I am diluting my focus and taking opportunities away from others on the team."*

Give them another way to accomplish their goal. If the first step made it clear that the work needs to be done and the second step made it clear that you won't be the one doing it, help your teammate figure out who will. For example, if you decide not to attend a sales meeting with a potential customer, you might say, *"What will it take to win this assignment?" "For whom on the team is this really their sweet spot?" "Who would be thrilled to get this opportunity?"*

Your teammates will find it refreshing when you have an authentic conversation with them about what you will and won't take on. It's much better than saying "yes" to something that you will never get around to or will do poorly because you're distracted and racing to finish. Just remember, you need to give the same courtesy to the people who say "no" to you.

HELP! IT DIDN'T WORK

Sometimes your attempts to say "no" won't work. You might have a boss like the one I had early in my career who insisted that everything was equally urgent. In that case, there are a few things you can do to reduce the impact of saying "yes" on your team.

Be explicit about the order in which you'll tackle the pile. Even if your boss plays hardball and expects you to deliver everything, you might get more information out of him if you declare your starting point. At least that way you'll have his endorsement for what got done first (and therefore what didn't).

Talk about priorities with your teammates. If your team leader refuses to prioritize and insists that everything is equally urgent, see if your teammates can shed any light on things. It's possible that one of the tasks is for a teammate who is willing to put their request at the bottom of the pile.

Warn people that you're overwhelmed. Saying "yes" is a risk to your team because you may let others down and leave them in a lurch. If you are worried that you're overcommitted with no way to say "no," give your teammates a heads-up and see if there is anything they can do to help. Even if they can't help, they will be able to prepare and compensate.

Work smart. When you're really busy, you probably try to do three things at once. Unfortunately, that actually slows you down. If you have to deal with an excessive workload, make a prioritized list, close your e-mail, turn off your ringer, and start crossing one thing off at a time. Reward yourself with five-minute breaks and feel the heady rush of making progress.

People aren't always going to like hearing you say "no." But there are only 24 hours in a day and you can only get so much accomplished. Work smart, do what you can, and make sure you minimize the impact of your unmanageable workload on your teammates.

Times to Say "Yes"

Of course, there's an exception that proves every rule. There are legitimate and important exceptions to the rule of saying "no." Remember, you're a member of a team and not everything is going to be neat and tidy all the time. Sometimes you need to say "yes," deliberately, knowingly, even when things are outside of your sweet spot.

Emergencies. If there is something major going down on your team, now is not the time to lecture your teammates about being crisis junkies and then return to your well-thought-out list of priority tasks. Few things have made my blood boil more than a secretary in the Psychology Department when I was a student who had a patronizing little sign above her desk that read: "An absence of planning on your part does not constitute an emergency on my part." If it's a crisis and your teammate needs you, get in there. Obviously, you need to address the issue when things calm down, but if your teammates, your customers, or your organization is at risk, don't sit up on a high horse while others are scrambling.

Grunt work. Let's face it, there are lots of things that need to be done at work that are not sexy, not glamorous, and not fun. Taking on your share of these tasks will do wonders for the culture and sense of camaraderie on your team. Do yourself a favor and learn how to use the photocopier. Then if you ever end up with a little too much work to do and you need to finish something after hours at the office, you won't need to keep an administrative assistant there with you. You could even put your own cup in the dishwasher—but now I'm talking crazy.

Saying "yes" is important when it's the right work and you're the right person. It's also a good thing in a very select set of other circumstances. But every "yes" to something new dilutes the things you have already committed to. If you feel badly when you say "no," remember that you are reaffirming the things that are important. Every "no" is a "yes" to your other priorities.

If you change what you say "yes" to, you'll change your team.

HEALTH CHECK: DO YOU KNOW WHEN TO SAY "NO?"

If you are fighting the urge to say "yes" and getting comfortable with your responsibility to Know When to Say "No," you're supposed to say "yes" to the points in the test in Figure 12.1. How are you doing?

Responsibilities		Yes
Unimportant Items	I encourage my team to set clear priorities.	☐
	I ask for clarification about where new tasks fit in priority order.	☐
	I question whether work needs to be done at all.	☐
	I occasionally check to see that tasks are still relevant.	☐
	I question tasks that emerge in a crisis rather than jumping right in.	☐
Not Your Role	I turn down work that is not in my sweet spot.	☐
	I refrain from adding value if it's value someone else should be adding.	☐
	I delegate work that can be done well by others more junior than me.	☐
	I distribute work that can be done more effectively by others.	☐
	I ask for help when I'm not capable of doing work effectively or efficiently.	☐
Not Quite "No"	I ask about the purpose of work before diving in.	☐
	I delay work to focus on fewer priorities at a time.	☐
	I push back when I believe work could be done more efficiently.	☐
	I ask questions to understand the level of quality required in outputs.	☐
	I make sure not to overdo the quality of work as my default or all the time.	☐
Saying "No" Nicely	I say "no" to my teammates when they ask me to do inappropriate work.	☐
	I help my teammates question the value of proposed activities.	☐
	I share my priorities with others so they know what I am saying "yes" to.	☐
	I find an appropriate person to help with work I shouldn't assist with.	☐
	I understand when my teammates say "no" to some requests I make.	☐

Figure 12.1   When to Say "No" Health Check Test

YOUR RESPONSIBILITY IN REVIEW

1. Wanting to say "yes" can cause you to be spread too thin, which is bad for you and for your team.

   - Wanting to fit in is natural, because you never want to miss out, but it's dangerous.

   - The sense of obligation to your teammates can cause you to say "yes" in an effort to pull your weight as a member of the team.

   - Genuine interest and curiosity can cause you to bite off more than you can chew.

   - Bad leaders are also responsible when they fail to prioritize and create unmanageable workloads.

2. You need to know when to say "no."

   - Understand your *sweet spot*: the intersection of things you were hired to do, that you're great at, and that are a priority for your team.

   - Say "no" to the work that is *irrelevant* or that can be *delayed*.

   - Find the appropriate person and *distribute* work that is important, but not in your sweet spot. Focus on activities where you are adding *unique value* that others can't add.

   - *Say "no" nicely* by helping your teammates question the necessity of work.

   - Reduce the negative impact when your boss *won't take "no" for an answer*. Make sure your teammates are aware of your predicament.

3. Say "yes" when it makes sense.

   - Do your part when there's a *crisis* and save your concerns for the postmortem.

   - Take on your fair share of the *grunt work* to show that you are one of the team and willing to roll up your sleeves.

CHAPTER 13

Embrace Productive Conflict

You find yourself sitting in the cafeteria talking about a proposed new product line with two teammates. You had a long to-do list, but these two have grabbed you and it doesn't look like they're going to let go anytime soon. The person doing most of the talking is Frank, a senior member of the team with many years' experience and strong influence over the boss. The other person is Lisa, one of your good friends on the team with whom you have been developing a plan for a new set of products.

The conversation began innocently enough when Frank asked you and Lisa for an update on your project. Once it became clear that you weren't going to appease Frank with quick answers to his questions, the three of you found a table and settled into a discussion.

After a few minutes of relatively innocuous questions, you realize Frank is holding back. His body language suggests he is uncomfortable and that there's something he isn't saying. Finally, he comes around to an issue you know is going to be a sticky one: The proposed new product line you are championing will mean finally abandoning an old line that Frank has been trying unsuccessfully to get off the ground for two years. The people he needs to keep that product alive are the same ones you'll need for the initial stages of your project. Moving them to the new project will cut off the last vestiges of hope that the old product can succeed.

Frank goes on the offensive. *"I'm asking you not to present your plan at the team meeting on Friday. I want six more months to prove that the A300 line is a winner. I know what we've been missing and I'm going to present my plan on Friday for how I'll turn it around."* You are a little taken aback; did he really just ask you to withdraw your plan? He chimes in again before you have time to collect your thoughts.

"I've spoken with Phillipe, Mo, and Sharon and they are all onside with giving the A300 another go." Lisa isn't saying anything; she's just watching in disbelief.

What do you do?

Think about situations you've had on your own team. Which of the following four endings is most likely for you?

A: You listen and ask a few questions, and then tell Frank that you think it's important for the whole team to discuss the options at the meeting on Friday.

or

B: You relent and ask only for a skeleton staff to do a feasibility test so that Frank can keep the people he needs for the next six months to implement his new plan.

or

C: You make nice with Frank in the moment and then quietly lobby members of the team to support your initiative at the meeting on Friday.

or

D: You go on the offensive and launch into a litany of reasons why your plan is better for the team and better for the company than continuing to throw good money after bad on the A300.

Would you choose ending A? Would you take the high road and work collaboratively toward the best solution for the team? Or is ending B more like you? Would you cave and let Frank have his way without ever putting the question to the team? How about ending C? Would you take the cowardly route and fight for your plan guerilla-style behind closed doors? Or would you choose ending D? Would you attack with a well-planned offense, not worrying about who gets hurt in the process? You don't need to tweet your answer to the world, but you do need to be honest with yourself about your default conflict style.

The truth is that only a small minority can say they regularly choose ending A. Most people follow one of the other three paths instead of taking the high road and having a fair, mature, and transparent conversation about which is the right plan for the team and the company. Conflict is our greatest Achilles' heel on teams.

WE STINK AT CONFLICT

Conflict. Does the very mention of the word make you uncomfortable? Or do you see it as an unpleasant but important part of life? If you actually think conflict is fun, a sport even, I'll get to you later. For most people, conflict doesn't feel good, and it's probably not how you would choose to spend your day. Some teams ask me not to use the word *conflict* at all: *"Can we just say 'disagreement,' or 'difference of opinion'?"* These are usually the same people who won't talk about weaknesses, only "opportunities for development." If everything for you is an opportunity for development, this chapter is going to be a tough row to hoe.

The problem is that the word *conflict* brings to mind the personal, exhausting tugs of war that I refer to as unproductive conflict. Unproductive conflict goes back and forth (and around and around) because no one is listening to anyone else and no one will budge from their original positions. In an effort to intimidate or bully the opponent into changing their position, the combatants get nasty and desperate. The result of fearing aggressive, nasty conflict is that many teams avoid having conflict directly and instead engage in hidden conflict in the form of gossip, backstabbing, and resistance.

That's unproductive conflict, too.

The alternative to unproductive conflict isn't hidden conflict; it's open, productive conflict. Productive conflict means you and your teammates move forward by engaging and struggling with different aspects of an issue to come to a good solution. You know you're having productive conflict because people are listening; they're being open-minded, and creative about solutions.

You might think that as a person who works with toxic executive teams, I spend the majority of my time working with groups who have too much conflict. Sometimes I do work with teams that want a referee to help manage conflict that has become vicious and personal. Much more often, I encounter teams whose dysfunction stems from their fear and avoidance of conflict. Because they're squeamish about disagreeing openly, they either squelch dissent completely and become a Bobble Head team, or they drive the conflict underground and become a Bleeding Back team. Too little conflict is a much bigger problem for teams than too much.

WHY WE DON'T FIGHT THE GOOD FIGHT

There are so many reasons, both personal and situational, why we don't use conflict as the positive force for progress and innovation that it can be. Understanding why you engage in unproductive conflict will put you in a better position to change your stripes. These reasons can be classified into five main categories. The first three lead you to suppress or hide conflict; the last two cause you to have destructive conflict.

Belief That Conflict Should Be Avoided

Some people believe intellectually that conflict of any kind is bad. Maybe you take a philosophical stance that harmonious relations are the way that civilization is supposed to work. You believe that we have risen above the other animals on the planet and, as humans, we should be able to get along without needing to fight with one another.

Or maybe it's self-preservation; you've learned the hard way not to have confidence in your ability to win in a fight. If you were teased in school or pushed around by an older sibling, you might have spent a lifetime learning how to fly below the radar to avoid having to fight.

If you work in an environment full of bullies, avoiding conflict and going with the flow may look like the safest route.

Alternatively, negative experiences or bad role models might have soured your view of conflict. If you have had an abusive boss who whipped up conflict among the members of your team or if you've been in a situation where team members have turned on one of their own, you might go to great lengths to avoid similar situations in the future.

Whether it's because you don't believe in it, because you don't think you can succeed through it, or because you don't think it can lead to a better outcome, you've probably got good reasons for avoiding conflict. The problem is that you're on a slippery slope that leads to a pit of groupthink and risky uniformity. You are going to have to open yourself to the benefits of healthy conflict.

Politeness and Saving Face

Some people don't necessarily eschew conflict; they just don't confront disagreements directly. You might be the kind of person who wants to preserve civility or a sense of decorum in the workplace. It's awkward to criticize someone's work or point of view, particularly in front of other people. As a result, you save your concerns for a more discreet forum. If you choose to share your concerns or criticism with the person in private, politeness might be an acceptable defense. But if you go straight to gossiping about people's ideas behind their backs, your politeness defense is a sham.

Team members who cling to their self-images as good, nice, friendly members of the team are just as likely to be at fault in an unhealthy team as their aggressive, combative colleagues are. That's because when you shy away from open, healthy conflict about the issues, the conflict pops up somewhere else. You are human, and if you try to suppress concern, frustration, or anger for too long, it's almost certain to erupt in an uncontrolled and ugly way at some point. Maybe it will emerge in a forked-tongue comment about your teammate or in an outburst of temper when you've been pushed past the breaking point. Worse, maybe you eventually quit without anyone ever knowing what was bothering you. You need to accept that it is neither polite, nor nice, nor productive to stay quiet about your concerns.

Lack of Courage

Your unwillingness to have conflict directly might be less about preserving the dignity of your teammates and more about protecting your own credibility and self-esteem. If you don't have strong evidence to support your concerns or your points of view—if your opinions are emotional and ungrounded—it might be easier not to raise them in the open where they can be examined and challenged. Instead, you might keep your thoughts to yourself until you're with a supportive audience. If you are always lobbing grenades from the safety of the bushes, you'll never earn the credibility on your team to have your ideas taken seriously.

Self-Preservation

Some people have no issue with conflict; quite the contrary, they think it's great sport. Unfortunately, these people manufacture unproductive, nasty conflict. You might see conflict as a win-lose proposition and therefore put significant energy into ensuring you're the winner, not the loser. You give up on issues and facts and start hurling insults or ripping scabs off old wounds. I have often found team members discussing situations that happened 5 or even 10 years previously. Get over it! If you see conflict as an adversarial process, you need to reframe it as a two-way dialogue rather than a one-way offensive.

Unfortunately, some organizations force people into this self-preservation mode. There are still plenty of organizations that present promotional opportunities as a battle to the death between two formerly friendly teammates: the so-called up-or-out strategy. If your boss runs her own version of the Hunger Games, seeing conflict as a zero-sum game might be the obvious, accurate conclusion.

Lack of Control

Some people don't actually want to be vicious and win at all costs. You might actually be a really decent person most of the time. You might enter into a conversation calmly, but when your expectations aren't met or your ideas or plans are questioned, you might be overcome by your frustration or anger and lash out at members of your team. You lack the self-control to rein in your emotions when things get too heated. When you are too busy launching attacks, you aren't listening and you're not open to other perspectives.

This often emerges with people who think they are playing the devil's advocate role—but really they're just being the devil. Make sure you're adding value with your comments, not just finding an excuse to be difficult.

EMBRACE PRODUCTIVE CONFLICT

Conflict, which for the purposes of teamwork I define as "uncomfortable friction between differing points of view," is absolutely necessary for a healthy team. Teams run into problems when they don't have conflict or when they have unproductive conflict. Productive conflict must be (1) forward-moving rather than repetitive and circular, (2) issue-based rather than personal, and (3) overt and expressed rather than hidden or disguised. Your final responsibility as a member of a team is to Embrace Productive Conflict.

> Conflict: noun. The uncomfortable friction between differing points of view.

The lack of productive conflict is at the heart of many of the Toxic Teams from the first half of this book. Think of the Bobble Head teams that just don't have any conflict at all.

If this is true of your team, ask yourself why. Maybe there are no differing points of view; there is so little diversity on your team that all team members are perfectly aligned. If this is the case, you aren't living up to your responsibility to Amplify Other Voices. Remember, if there is no diversity on the team, it's your responsibility to bring it in from outside the team.

If you're on a Spectator team, there may be different points of view, but your team isn't pushing hard enough on issues to create friction. You aren't Adding Your Full Value. Either way, it's a recipe for stagnation, and stagnation creates risk. I once bought a fridge magnet that said, "Even if you're on the right track, if you sit there long enough, you'll get run over." That's what happens when your team has no conflict. You can use the tactics in the rest of this chapter to change the way your team views conflict.

In Bleeding Back teams, there is conflict—it's just hidden. People nod and agree in meetings and then have conflict outside the room. Maybe one person quietly shirks his commitments and fails to take action. Maybe multiple team members gossip or betray one another's trust. Sometimes your team leader is complicit, allowing team members to use back channels to revisit decisions that have already been made.

It's similar to the Crisis Junkie team that waits for an emergency to short-circuit conflict, coming to an answer without really working through the issues. In both cases, you can use the techniques in the remainder of this chapter to get conflict on the agenda and give dissent a legitimate time and place to surface.

In Royal Rumble teams, conflict is personal and ugly. You are caught up in a wave of passion and emotion and not getting the most out of anyone on your team. It's so bad that you can't see a way out. Half the team is yelling and pounding tables (the "fight" side) while the other half is pushing their chairs away or looking at their smartphones (the "flight" side). Clearly, no one has Started with a Positive Assumption in months. You will definitely find the skills and language of productive conflict useful.

THE PATH FORWARD

There is a path forward. Your team will get comfortable with conflict—and by that I mean that you will get comfortable being uncomfortable. For most people, Embracing Productive Conflict is the toughest of your responsibilities as a team member. It's also the one that will make the biggest difference to you and your team.

Mind-Set of Productive Conflict: Two Truths

The most important idea to get your head around to create healthy, productive conflict is that you can be in conflict with someone without invalidating their opinion. You do this by accepting that there can be two truths in a situation. Of course, there can be 3, 4, or 72 truths, but the big leap is accepting that there is more than one— more than just yours.

This concept is really important in today's complex business world. Give credence to each way of looking at an issue—at least for the purpose of the argument. Clinging to one single truth, and fighting over whose truth is right, stifles possibility and creates a downward spiral. You won't make forward progress until you can reframe the situation and see it in new ways. Just because you're right doesn't mean the other person is wrong.

For example, I worked with a global bank where a team member in international wealth management got into a heated debate with the risk management person, saying, essentially, *"We have got to invest in country A. We need 200 percent growth in 18 months. You have no clue!"*

The risk management person came right back with, *"We can't invest there. We can't take on that much risk.* You *have no clue!"*

This debate over growth versus risk management was set up to be adversarial from the start. When two people act like only one of them can be right, they spend most of their time going back and forth—and little time going forward. That's not a very productive conversation. When they wrestled with the statement "We need to grow *and* manage risk," the tenor of the conversation changed completely.

If you name both viewpoints as true, everyone can relax and focus on coming up with a solution. If your team is stuck in a one-truth conflict, try writing the two truths on a whiteboard. It's amazing how writing something down makes people feel validated.

Two truths, one solution. Productive Conflict.

Get Conflict on the Table

Once you have embraced the idea that having different perspectives on the truth leads you to more effective and more innovative solutions, you need to create a forum to air those different perspectives in front of the team. Here are strategies to help you do so:

Set the tone. At the start of a meeting, conversation, or e-mail, be direct about your desire to have open and transparent conflict. Try saying, *"I'm concerned that we aren't using our meetings effectively to air all of our opinions."* Or *"I think it would be great if everyone could add value in the meeting, rather than raising important points after the meeting."* Continue that theme when a contentious issue comes up by saying, *"This is a sensitive discussion and it's one we need to have out in the open"* or *"I think we need to know how people are thinking about this. Would everyone weigh in on this, please?"*

Make room for dissent. Before the team makes a decision, create another opportunity for your teammates to air their opinions. Ask, *"Are we ready to make this decision?"* or *"What could we consider that would improve the quality of this decision?"* If it works and one of your teammates raises a contentious point of view, remember your responsibility to Amplify Other Voices and encourage the team to spend some time on it. *"That is a really different way of looking at this issue; what can we gain from that perspective?"* Before bringing a discussion to a close, ask, *"What are we not talking about?"* or *"If someone were to criticize this idea, what might they say?"* There are many opportunities to keep the discussion open and resist the tendency to converge too quickly. Use these opportunities to make room for differing points of view.

Call out bad behaviors. If your team is susceptible to passive-aggressive conflict, you can draw attention to it and make it much less common. When body language is negative, ask, *"I'm noticing that you're pushing away from the table. What are you thinking about?"* or *"I just saw three people roll their eyes. What's up?"* As I discussed in Chapter 11, you have to be really attentive to attempts to shut down healthy debate with humor. If you see that happening, call it out.

Shut down back channels. If members of your team are uncomfortable with conflict and there is an obvious and accessible alternative to dealing with it publicly, they will probably take it. You need to shut down those other avenues so conflict stays where it needs to be—out in the open. When a team member comes to complain outside the meeting, redirect them. *"I'm concerned that we didn't hear this point of view in the meeting. What are you hoping to accomplish by raising it now?" "I'm curious about your decision not to raise this in the team meeting."* If your teammate was anxious about raising an unpopular point, you can offer to support him in raising it in the next meeting—even if you don't agree, you can agree that the point needs to be considered.

If you are a team leader, it's your responsibility not to allow decisions to be reopened through back channels. When someone tries to reopen a decision, don't bite. *"What new information do we have that would lead us to reopen this decision?" "This decision has already been made; do you believe we need to take it back to the team?"*

No matter what role you play on a team, you can help get conflict out of the shadows and into the light where the parties involved have an opportunity to make their case and learn from one another. It might be uncomfortable and it might make you squirm, but I'm telling you that you need to do it anyway. Eat your conflict vegetables—they're good for you!

Use the Right Words

Finesse will help you raise a conflicting point of view without it starting World War III. If you choose your words carefully with the intention of making yourself clear and focusing on the issue, you will greatly reduce the resistance and defensiveness you trigger. Don't think of this as sugarcoating or pulling punches. If you do either, you've missed the point entirely. Instead, be direct and respectful as you discuss difficult topics. The following tips will help you choose the right words:

"But" out. The two-truths language comes from improvisational comedy, where actors are trained to use "and" as a way of always leaving a path for their partners to continue the sketch. Shutting people down doesn't make for entertaining improv and it doesn't make for good teams. My friends at Second City Communications do a fabulous job teaching people in corporate environments to use "yes, and" rather than "yes, but" in their interactions. The minute you use the word *but*, you're back to the single-truth version of the world.

One caveat: For all of you who have learned the "and"-instead-of-"but" technique, I need to tell you that a sanctimonious "aaaaaaaaaaaand" that you labor over for four seconds is not making things better. Say it because you mean it. *"It's going to be really tricky to figure out a way forward because you made a good point and I made a good point. We're smart, let's figure this out."*

What if? If you don't feel comfortable being assertive or disagreeing directly with your teammates, try asking them to imagine a different scenario. Imagine you're trying to plan a sales campaign to bring your services to a new segment of the market. You pitch your idea and your colleague immediately reacts with, *"We'll never find people who want to do door-to-door in those areas."* If you don't have counterevidence at hand, try a what-if scenario. *"I hear your concern about getting the right salespeople to pull off this campaign. If we could get the right people, what would the campaign look like?"* Your teammate might be more willing to entertain the conversation because she will always have the out that it was all hypothetical.

Impact. If your teammate shares a plan that you disagree with, you can say so directly, but that might cause her to get her back up. Instead of disagreeing with the plan, help your teammate think through the consequences by asking good open-ended questions about the impact. *"Okay, we're contemplating launching this product to only our U.S. customers. How is that going to land with our two big customers in Europe?"*

It's much nicer to be asked a question than to have an accusation lobbed at you. Imagine the difference if you had said, *"That's a really risky plan; it ignores our two big customers in Europe."* It's also worth noting the important difference between saying *"we're contemplating"* and *"you're contemplating."* That's the difference between *"we're in this together"* and *"you're on your own, sucker."*

Underlying issue. If you strongly disagree with a proposed action and you're fighting the negative assumption about your teammate's intentions or intelligence, start by trying to understand where he is coming from. Maybe you can find another way to accomplish the same goal. If your colleague says he wants to release the individual sales figures to the whole team, and your immediate thought is that you'll have half the team in your office in tears because they're failing and the other half demanding more money because they are succeeding, stay curious. *"I'm surprised you suggested we release the sales figures to the whole team. What is your goal in doing that?"* Again, don't be disingenuous. Be honest about the fact that you're surprised and then be open to good reasons why releasing sales figures might be the right thing to do.

Zip it and listen. The reason conflict becomes unproductive and goes around and around is that too few people actually listen to what the other parties in the discussion are saying. There's no point in asking great questions if you aren't going to listen to the answers. At the most superficial level, you need to make sure you understand the facts properly. When you're confused by the argument someone is making, ask for clarification. *"I am hearing two different issues in what you're saying. Am I hearing you correctly?"* Getting straight on how words are being used is also a good way to listen actively. *"You used the word 'resources.' What are you thinking of when you say 'resources'?"*

Once you are listening to and understanding the facts, you can key in on the emotions that might be making the conversation more heated than normal. Mention both the verbal and nonverbal cues you're picking up and see if you're interpreting your teammate accurately. *"You used the word 'important' several times in your presentation. I'm sensing that you feel very strongly about this issue." "As you were talking, your voice got louder and louder. How are you feeling about me bringing this issue forward?*

Last, you need to listen to what's not being said. By listening for the values and beliefs underlying your teammate's comments, you will get a sense of what might be fueling the conflict. *"I heard you say 'risky' a couple of times. What is this discussion triggering for you?" "It feels like this is at odds with how you think things should work. What do you think is important to protect here?"*

Thinking carefully about how you approach a delicate topic or a precarious situation will greatly increase the likelihood that you will contribute to a positive and constructive discussion with your team. Find ways to incorporate these words into your next disagreement. You'll notice the difference both in how it feels for you and in how your teammates respond.

Micro-Conflict—Embracing Productive Feedback

Recently, I took a team through our team effectiveness process. Before the third session, my colleague Janet and I had conducted interviews with the team to understand what issues they wanted to tackle during the session. One comment really struck me. One of the team members said they hoped that through the session the team could to learn to be "brutally honest" with one another.

There it was—the answer to their conflict aversion was right in front of me. In their minds, conflict was "brutal." This was a team of some of the nicest human beings I have ever worked with. As healthcare professionals, they're committed to their very important work of caring for some of the most fragile people in our society. I understood immediately why the team had struggled to embrace conflict: They thought of feedback, candor, and authenticity as brutal.

Feedback is the most basic form of perceived conflict—at least unsolicited feedback is. Healthy, productive teams believe that feedback is precious and that it is helpful. They understand that the feedback is there to help them grow. Their attitude toward feedback is in stark contrast to people who believe it's "not nice" to say something negative about a person. People who Embrace Productive Conflict believe that it's not nice to see someone go off the rails and *not* say something, just like it's not nice to see me with spinach in my teeth and to let me go to two important meetings without saying something. The most important thing is your intent in giving feedback and how you deliver the feedback to optimize the impact.

When you see a teammate do something that you believe is harmful to themselves or to the team, your mind-set needs to be one of assistance. *"I don't know if she realizes how that came across. I should help her understand how it sounded." "I would want someone to tell me if I were in the same situation."* It's also important not to make it a catastrophe. Your mind-set should be positive and supportive.

As you probably know from an unpleasant episode where you got in trouble trying to be helpful, it's not enough to have a positive intent. You have to think about how to deliver your feedback so that it lands positively. Frame your feedback by talking about the situation. Use specific, behavioral observations, not judgments, and then share the impact you think the behavior had. Last, open up the conversation so the person can respond.

"Jean, when we were discussing Marie's new project and you gave reasons why it wouldn't work before she finished describing the approach, the team stopped listening to Marie before she could show that she had addressed the issues. How do you think this might have affected Marie?"

"When you were presenting your update to the team and you used 27 slides for a 20-minute presentation, I saw several people pull out their

phones. I felt bad that the real progress wasn't appreciated. How could you emphasize your key points differently next time?"

There aren't too many people who enjoy getting constructive feedback in the moment. Most of us like to preserve the illusion that we did a good job. But over the long run, people come to trust and rely on the people who care enough about them and have enough courage to deliver tough feedback. They would never describe what their teammates offer as "brutal honesty." Instead, they experience it as genuine, supportive honesty. And that kind of honesty means your teammates have got your back.

A conflict-avoidant culture or poor conflict skills are a key part of every Toxic Team. If you are living in some delusional state pretending everything will be fine if you all just get along, you are putting your team in jeopardy. It's time to change the way you think about conflict. Start thinking of conflict as a positive and progressive part of your team interactions. If you can change your mind-set, you won't have difficulty making the time and space for disagreements. You'll be motivated to engage in conflict with words that are constructive rather than with sloppy language that makes everything unclear or unpleasant. As you get comfortable being uncomfortable, you'll be able to dial up the feedback and everyone on your team will get better quickly. Otherwise, you're just sitting on the track waiting to get run over.

If you change the way you disagree, you'll change your team.

HEALTH CHECK: ARE YOU EMBRACING PRODUCTIVE CONFLICT?

If you are getting comfortable being uncomfortable, you shouldn't feel conflicted about the items in the test in Figure 13.1. How are you doing?

Responsibilities		Yes
Conflict Mind-Set	I see conflict as an important part of a healthy team.	☐
	I confront difficult conversations directly and with courage.	☐
	I talk about multiple perspectives being true.	☐
	I stay open and curious about different points of view.	☐
	I work with my teammates to solve for two truths when there's a disagreement.	☐
Forum for Conflict	I ask my teammates to raise their concerns publicly.	☐
	I inquire about different opinions before making a decision.	☐
	I call it out when my teammates are shutting down conflict.	☐
	I don't allow my teammates to gossip to me.	☐
	I ask for issues raised outside the team to be put back on the agenda.	☐
The Right Words	I have stopped saying "yes, but" when responding to my colleagues.	☐
	I use what-if questions to help my teammates move beyond conflict.	☐
	I help teammates to understand the impact of proposed actions.	☐
	I ask questions to understand the rationale behind plans I disagree with.	☐
	I wait and listen to my teammates' responses after asking questions.	☐
Embracing Feedback	I see giving feedback as part of my responsibility to my teammates.	☐
	I make feedback concrete and share observations to make it objective.	☐
	I provide my perspective on the impact of my teammates' behavior.	☐
	I am careful in how I construct feedback so it feels respectful.	☐
	I ask my teammates to provide feedback to help me improve.	☐

Figure 13.1   Embrace Productive Conflict Health Check Test

YOUR RESPONSIBILITY IN REVIEW

1. Nasty interpersonal conflict can cripple a team. So can fearing or avoiding conflict altogether.

   - Some teams avoid conflict and risk creating a dangerous groupthink situation.

   - Passive-aggressive teams, whether because of politeness, lack of courage, or self-preservation, don't deal with conflict directly but allow it to fester beneath the surface.

   - Aggressive, immature teams make conflict personal.

2. You need to embrace productive conflict.

   - See conflict as a process of solving for *two truths*, rather than as a fight over one single truth.

   - Create the *forum for conflict* to happen in the open so that issues can be identified and addressed. Set the tone in meetings, make room for dissent, call out bad behaviors, and shut down back channels so conflicts are forced onto the table.

   - Use deliberate and *positive language* to demonstrate curiosity and reduce defensiveness. Listen and respond based on what you hear.

3. Provide feedback continuously.

   - View feedback as a *positive contribution* to the success of your teammates and the health of your team.

   - Make your feedback *concrete and behavioral* and share not only the behavior, but the impact that the behavior had on you and others.

CHAPTER 14

You First

Building a healthy and productive team is crucial and it's possible. If you are just forming a new team, now you have the daily regimen that will allow you to start things off on the right foot. When you start out by paying attention to your five responsibilities as a team member, you will form healthy habits that will inoculate your team against dysfunction.

Don't kid yourself: You will encounter stress and tensions. But if you approach them with a positive attitude and a willingness to focus on the issue and work to the best solution, you'll slowly build the confidence that your team can tackle whatever comes at you. You can build a great team.

Even more important, there is a path back from mediocrity and even from outright dysfunction if you're on a Toxic Team. Making the personal changes required to change your assumptions, add your full value, amplify other voices, say "no" more deliberately, and engage in productive conflict will allow you to lead the change on your team. Bringing in the structural and process supports outlined in the triage sections in the first half of the book will bolster your individual efforts and start to embed the changes in the way you do things as a team. I know it can be done because I've seen it work— over and over.

Let's go back to the Toxic Team from Chapter 2—you remember the executive team of the small financial organization, the "rabies shot" team. Things had spiraled downward over several months to the point where no one could make eye contact. In their interviews, they'd told us stories of mistrust and vicious rivalry that had started to seep down into the layers of the organization. It was an ugly situation.

Today, you would never know that team had been through such agony. They know what it feels like to dislike and mistrust their teammates, and be disliked and mistrusted in return, and they are willing to make the investment day after day to ensure they never get back there again. They still argue; in fact, they've enshrined their own code of conduct around conflict, which they refer to in boxing parlance as "in the ring time," to remind them to keep their conflict above the belt and in the ring. If anything, they have more conflict now because they have the trust required to disagree without the fear of making things worse.

It was our third session with them when everything changed for the better. One member of the team, the CFO, realized that he was contributing to the problem. He raised his hand and said, "I have to take ownership of my part in this. I realize I'm grabbing the reins and not leaving you room to prove to me you're capable. For my part, I promise to give you more room to do your jobs." It was a big moment. The team had entered the room expecting that they would have a rock-'em-sock-'em, no-holds-barred battle, and here was the bully CFO short-circuiting it all with a heartfelt admission that he was a part of the problem.

What do you think happened next? Pile on the CFO? *"You're right, you* were *a jerk!"* No, not at all. Instead, the next person to speak was the VP of HR, one of the people who had been most affected by the CFO's lack of confidence in the team. She quickly took on her share of the responsibility for what had gone wrong: "I was hurt when you didn't trust me to do that work, but I shouldn't have responded by shutting you out. I'm sorry." By that point, the tide was unstoppable. One team member after another stepped up and took ownership for what they needed to change.

In fact, all of the Toxic Teams in the first half of the book made significant progress toward being more effective for their organizations and more rewarding for their members. The process we worked through together helped them understand how their behavior contributed to dysfunction. But without a single individual on each team who wanted to make things different, I would not have been able to make change happen. Remember, I don't have a magic wand, just a mirror.

One individual on each of those teams had the courage and the resolve to make things better. Becky from the Bleeding Back team in Chapter 6 stands out. She was the one who finally put a stop to back-channel gossip by responding to an e-mail with the simple words, "We agreed that we don't want to be like this anymore." Her response garnered respect and thanks from her teammates who had not yet internalized how things needed to change. She started the ball rolling.

Russell made the difference on the team in Chapter 5 with Spectator issues. After watching his boss fly through multiple agenda items with no time for discussion among the members of his team, Russell politely and firmly told the team leader that the meeting format wasn't meeting his needs. "I'm not comfortable making this decision without hearing from everyone. This project will require everyone's participation to be successful and I think it's worth the investment to get their input now." He was the first to stand up to the boss, but not the last.

In every successful team intervention, you can pinpoint the exact moment when the team starts to turn the corner. It's the second that the first person really gets it. You'll see the look on their face. Usually it's a quiet moment. The person disengages from the group discussion, momentarily consumed by the conversation in their head. *"I can't be a part of this anymore. This is about me. If we're going to fix anything, I'm going to have to go first."* When the person re-engages in the conversation, the tone changes. Suddenly their sentences start with "I." They take personal responsibility for doing things differently.

It doesn't have to be as dramatic as a personal admission of guilt. You can just start acting differently. You will say plenty by changing the tone of your voice, using questions instead of asserting yourself, and staying open and curious about what your teammates are really trying to convey. It might take a little while for your teammates to notice that something is different, but they will notice.

The person who goes first has tremendous power.

Once you declare your unwillingness to continue with the patterns that got your team to where it is, it will be very difficult for others on your team to persist in their bad behavior. Some of your teammates will come along with you immediately. Other teammates will wait to see if things are really going to change. Just keep going. They'll join in once they know it's for real. Unfortunately, one or two teammates might continue their counterproductive behavior. The good news is that they will stick out like sore thumbs.

Here's why it works. If each member of your team who is committed to changing things for the better refuses to engage with the naysayers, they will soon have nowhere to turn. If you refuse to listen to gossip, the negative message will lose its audience. If you respond to hostility with calmness and curiosity about what's really going on, the aggressor will be hard-pressed to manufacture a fight. If you make room for the voices they are trying to stifle, the majority will suddenly be in the minority. In many cases, your team leader will be compelled to remove the persistent naysayer from the team. In other cases, the bad apple will stay, but you'll get whatever value is there and contain the negative impact of their behavior.

Sadly, it doesn't work with every team. I still carry with me the profound disappointment in a few teams where no one had the guts to make a change. Sure, they went through the motions and talked a good game about how they were going to change, but it was clear that they hadn't made the commitment to doing things differently. Often the problem was the team leader. In the rare cases where things don't improve on a team, it's usually the team leader that is holding the team back. Bad team leaders doom the team to perpetual dysfunction because they're not willing to confront the things they do that are harmful.

If you find yourself on a team where people aren't willing to create a healthy and productive environment, get out. If you've tried to make things better, taken responsibility for your own contribution to the problem, and helped your teammates see how it could be different—don't waste your life in a bad situation. It's not worth it.

A healthy and vital team is a goal worth striving for. You will know it when you get there—just picture it. You walk into work every Monday with clarity about what your team exists to do and your exact role in making it happen. In fact, you don't mind signing in to your e-mail on Sunday night just so you're ready to get a jump start on the week. At work, you make a meaningful contribution that is complemented by the value you get from your teammates. When you go to a team meeting, you know that you're going to learn something you didn't know when you walked in. You're relieved when your teammates help you spot issues and opportunities you hadn't thought of, and your teammates are grateful when you reciprocate with ideas about their work. Getting things done is easy, and you feel a sense of accomplishment when you pack up to go home.

It's not all smiles and singing "Kumbaya." You feel tension sometimes, but it's the tension that comes from pushing yourselves to accomplish more. Your team is ambitious and you struggle and wrestle and challenge one another to make things better and better. Your team has conflict, but it's almost always honest, productive debate about the issues. When conflict does get personal, you and your teammates catch yourselves, apologize, and go back to talking about the issues. You trust and respect your teammates enough to accept their apologies and to move on without holding a grudge. You know that you're on a healthy team because being with your teammates charges your batteries rather than draining them.

Is it worth it? Are you ready to change your team?

The good news is that you don't have to go it alone. You might be the only person on your team who realizes that things need to change, but there are other people in other organizations who are making the difference on their teams, too. I've created a place for you to connect with those people and to commiserate, get ideas, and recommit to the difficult but important process of making things better. That place is the www.ChangeYourTeam.com community.

If you're seriously considering having a go at changing your team, the website is filled with resources and tools to help you get started. There you can read about topics from the book in greater depth and print out worksheets to plan your approach to living up to your five responsibilities. You can also ask me questions and share your stories. Most important, you can connect with other brave souls like you who are making the investment in themselves and their teams.

You can make a huge difference. Living up to your responsibilities as a team member will lift a weight from your shoulders. You will feel great about yourself knowing that you are contributing to a healthier and more productive team. Your new attitude will be obvious to your friends and your family. They will see it on your face when you walk through the door. Your example will inspire your teammates to behave better, too. It's all possible. They will follow, but *you first*.

NOTES

CHAPTER 1: CHANGE YOURSELF, CHANGE YOUR TEAM

1. Blanchard, K, (2007), *Leading at a Higher Level: Blanchard on Leadership and Creating High Performing Organizations*. Upper Saddle River, NJ: Prentice Hall.
2. Science Daily, "Groups Perform Better Than the Best Individuals at Solving Complex Problems," April 23, 2006, http://www.sciencedaily .com/releases/2006/04/060423191907.htm.
3. Charles Pavitt, "Chapter 2—Groups Versus Individuals: Which Is 'Better'?" in *Small Group Communication: A Theoretical Approach*, 3rd. ed., last modified September 24, 2008, www.uky.edu/~drlane/teams/pavitt/ word/ch2.doc.
4. Ian Sample, "Working in a Team Increases Human Pain Threshold," *Guardian*, September 15, 2009, http://www.guardian.co.uk/science/ 2009/sep/16/teams-do-better-research-proves.
5. Wolfgang Stroebe and Michael Diehl, (1994), "Why Groups Are Less Effective Than Their Members: On Productivity Losses in Idea-Generating Groups," *European Review of Social Psychology*, 5(1): 271–303.

CHAPTER 2: TOXIC TEAMS

1. The stories in this book are all based on experiences I've had working with teams. Given the sensitive nature of the content, I've disguised characters and situations, but I've stayed true to the issues that caused both the dysfunctions and the breakthroughs.

CHAPTER 3: THE CRISIS JUNKIE TEAM

1. Steven J. Karau and Janice R. Kelly, (2004), "Time, Pressure, and Team Performance: An Attentional Focus Integration," Sally Blount

(ed.), in *Time in Groups* (*Research on Managing Groups and Teams, Volume 6*), Emerald Group Publishing Limited, pp. 185–212.

CHAPTER 9: START WITH A POSITIVE ASSUMPTION

1. Daniel Goleman, (1995), *Emotional Intelligence: Why It Can Matter More than IQ* (New York: Bantam Books).

CHAPTER 11: AMPLIFY OTHER VOICES

1. The Birkman® Method tool is the one I use. It creates breakthroughs in team effectiveness. Learn more about it in *The Birkman Method: Your Personality at Work*. Sharon Birkman Fink and Stephanie Capparrell. Hoboken, NJ: John Wiley & Sons, 2013.

ACKNOWLEDGMENTS

A book like this is a mosaic of the amazing experiences I have had working with fabulous people on wonderful teams. To my clients, I am indebted for your confidence in me and your willingness to trust me with your most critical business issues and your most intimate personal vulnerabilities.

To David Shaw, the founder and CEO of Knightsbridge Human Capital Solutions, thank you for believing in me and for always making me feel like a key member of your team.

To all of my Knightsbridge colleagues, it is an honor to build a company with you. Special thanks to Leslie Carter, Lori Dyne, and Mirren Hinchley for your help in bringing *You First* to the world; to Victoria Davies for teaching me the financial and legal ropes; and to Dr. Ralph Shedletsky for your wisdom and your friendship.

Thank you to Dr. Nick Morgan, Nikki-Smith Morgan, Sarah Morgan, and Emma Wyatt of Public Words. You not only helped me tell my story, but you also helped me find my voice. I found so much value in your expertise and so much comfort in your friendship. Huge thanks to Peggy McEwan for bringing my ideas to life through her fantastic original artwork. You nailed it!

Sincere thanks to the staff at John Wiley & Sons who contributed greatly to this project. A special thank you is due to Shannon Vargo, Elana Schulman, and Karen Milner.

Thank you to Helen Lee for research assistance that got the early versions of this book rolling.

To the Knightsbridge Leadership Solutions team, I cannot tell you how it feels to experience the magic of being a part of your team. You are my colleagues, my sounding boards, my coaches, my friends—and you are the model for all that this book is about.

The shoemaker's children have shoes! To Colleen Ryan, who has made me look good for 14 years. To my leadership team colleagues, Audra August, Bryan Benjamin, Brian Wellman, Razia Garda, and especially Tammy Heermann, who teaches me every day about how to be a better team member.

Profound thanks to Dr. Vince Molinaro, who has been my trusted partner and sounding board for over 8 years. This book would not be what it is without you. Our team would not be what it is without you. Thank you for being my best advocate.

Writing this book while engaged as a business leader and an active consultant took the efforts and contributions of my whole village. Thank you to dear friends Tracey, Nancy, Stephanie, and Vickie for moments of respite. To the moms of Turning Pointe for helping me juggle priorities. Thank you to my parents, Joan and Garn; my in-laws, Betty and Leslie; and to the aunts and uncles, Scott, Harriet, Laura, and Raymond, who entertained my children so Mommy could write.

To my daughters, Kira and Mac—I love you so much and I'm so proud of you. I hope you experience the joy of being part of great teams throughout your lives.

To my husband, Craig—you inspire me, support me, challenge me, and love me. You are the best teammate of all.

ABOUT THE AUTHOR

Liane Davey, PhD combines her expertise in strategy with her deep insight into group dynamics to create powerful changes in top teams. As a Vice President of Knightsbridge Leadership Solutions and the Lead for Team effectiveness, she is sought out by executives at some of North America's leading financial services, consumer goods, high tech, and health care organizations.

She works to rehabilitate teams that have become toxic and with healthy teams that want to take their performance to the next level. To meet the needs of a broader audience, Liane has distilled her approach into Knightsbridge's highly successful Vital Teams^{TM} and Team Inoculation^{TM} programs. She has also built a program to allow organizations to certify their internal resources to deliver these programs.

A dynamic keynote speaker, Liane takes her message about vital teams to conferences and management retreats. In addition, she writes an ongoing blog on Team Effectiveness and is published in trade and academic journals.

Liane is a passionate advocate for mental health and brings her energy to the cause through roles as an evaluator for the Psychologically Healthy Workplace Awards and as a member of the Board of Trustees of the Psychology Foundation. She holds a PhD in Industrial/Organizational Psychology from the University of Waterloo. Liane is happily married with two young daughters.

Follow Liane on Twitter @LianeDavey

ABOUT KNIGHTSBRIDGE HUMAN CAPITAL SOLUTIONS

Knightsbridge is a unique human capital solutions company designed from the outset to be truly integrated—to seamlessly bring together a diverse group of experts to find, develop and optimize your people. Our consultants bring together their diverse expertise as a unified team, to provide our clients with deeper insight into their human capital needs and deliver more strategic, customized solutions based on an integrated view.

Across North America and around the world through our global partnerships with AMROP and The Career Star Group, Knightsbridge works with clients to seamlessly execute their strategy through people.

Knightsbridge has the people you need, when you need stronger people.

www.knightsbridge.com

Index

Disagreements. *See also* Royal Rumble team
  Bleeding Back team and, 81
  Bobble Head team and, 52
Disengagement, Spectator team and, 63
Dissent. *See also* Royal Rumble team
  making room for, Bleeding Back team and,
    82
  productive conflict and, 205
Diversity
  adding full value and, 144
  other voices and, 159–161, 168–169, 171
Dynamic problems, 18–19

Emanuel, Rahm, 27
Embarrassing behavior, Royal Rumble team
  and, 94
Emergencies, saying "yes" and, 190
Emotional intelligence, Royal Rumble team
  and, 91
Emotions, understanding, to promote positive
  assumptions, 126–127
Empathy, Royal Rumble team and, 99
Engagement, Royal Rumble team and, 89–90,
  94, 96
Exhaustion, not adding full value and, 135
Experience, leveraging to add full value,
  141–143
Expertise, obsession with, not adding full value
  and, 137

Face saving, conflict avoidance and, 199–200
Familiarity, Bobble Head team and, 45–46
Fear of missing out (FOMO), not saying "no"
  and, 177–178
Feedback
  lack of, Bleeding Back team and, 75
  productive conflict and, 209–211, 213
Feynmann, Richard, 162
Finesse, productive conflict and, 206–209, 213
Focus, lack of, not adding full value and, 136
FOMO (fear of missing out), not saying "no"
  and, 177–178
Full value, adding, 9, 108, 131–152
  adding wrong value, 148, 151–152
  causes of not adding value, 134–137, 151
  conflict and, 202
  health check for, 149–150
  inner circle and, 146–147
  responsibilities for improving team, 151–152
  techniques for, 138–144, 151
  vulnerability and, 145–146
Functions and roles, diversity and, 168

Goleman, Daniel, 121
Gossip, shutting down, Bleeding Back team
  and, 83
"Grunt work," saying "yes" and, 190

Health checks
  adding full value, 149–150
  amplifying other voices, 169–170
  embracing productive conflict, 211–212
  saying "no," 191
  starting with positive assumptions, 129
Homogeneity, Bobble Head team and, 46
Humor, Royal Rumble team and, 96–97

Impact of plan, productive conflict and,
  207–208
Implementation
  slow, Bleeding Back team and, 77
  struggles with, Spectator team and, 63
Industry expertise, adding full value and,
  141–143
Infighting, Crisis Junkie team and, 29–30
Information, gathering to promote positive
  assumptions, 123–126
Inner circle, breaking into, 146–147
Innovator's Dilemma, The (Christensen), 87
Integrity, of teammates, 126–128, 130
Inter-team confusion, Bleeding Back team and,
  77–78
Issues
  focusing on, Royal Rumble team and,
    98–99
  resolving, Crisis Junkie team and, 35–36
  underlying, productive conflict and, 208
Izzo, Dr. John, 10–11

Knee-jerk reactions, Crisis Junkie team and, 31

Life experience, adding full value and, 143
Listening, productive conflict and, 208–209

Mandates
  defining of, Crisis Junkie team and, 34
  developing of, Spectator team and, 65
  lack of, Spectator team and, 60–61
Meetings
  delegation and saying "no," 187
  fixing, Crisis Junkie team and, 34–35
  poor management of, Royal Rumble team
    and, 91–92
  resetting of, Spectator team and, 65, 66, 67
Micro-conflicts, 209–211

BRING THE POWER OF TEAM EFFECTIVENESS INTO YOUR ORGANIZATION

The You First Workshop

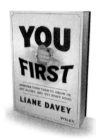

Based on the powerful ideas of the book *You First: Inspire Your Team to Grow Up, Get Along, and Get Stuff Done*, this interactive workshop will create individual accountability for team effectiveness. Great for retreats, town hall meetings, and annual kick-off sessions, the workshop will help employees diagnose the issues their teams are most susceptible to and to understand the role they play in preventing and fixing dysfunction. Your people will walk out of a room with the accountability and the skills to make their teams work.

Team Inoculation™—Immunize Your Teams from Dysfunction

Do you have a team that you want to set on the path to high performance? Don't rely on silly or superficial team building sessions. Make an investment in the success of the team. The one-day Knightsbridge Team Inoculation™ program is a perfect start for a new team or a booster shot for existing teams. The program starts with creating alignment around the mandate of the team, includes an individual assessment, and concludes with the team creating the rules of engagement for how they will work together.

Vital Teams™ Process—Rehabilitate Your Most Important Teams

Every organization has a few teams that can't afford to fail. Unfortunately, the pressure, urgency, and scrutiny can just make the normal human dynamics even more fragile. The Knightsbridge Vital Teams™ process is an in-depth, multimodule approach to getting teams back on track. The program builds team alignment around the team's business mandate, provides insight into the individual needs of team members, and addresses specific structural and behavioral challenges facing the team.

Change the trajectory of your teams today. To learn more about The You First workshop and our other team effectiveness programs go to www.knights bridge.com.